The Technique of
WOVEN TAPESTRY

Frontispiece
Tapestry in the making. Warp: cotton. Weft: worsted.
Worked in cheviot and crewel wool

The Technique of
WOVEN TAPESTRY

Tadek Beutlich

B T BATSFORD LTD   LONDON
WATSON-GUPTILL PUBLICATIONS   NEW YORK

First published 1967
Second impression 1969
Reprinted 1971
Reprinted 1972
Reprinted 1974

(UK)   ISBN 0 7134 2513 x
(USA) ISBN 0–8230–5300–8

Published 1967 by B T BATSFORD LTD
4 Fitzhardinge Street, London, W.1
Published 1967 by WATSON-GUPTILL PUBLICATIONS
Astor Plaza New York, New York 10036
No part of this book may be reproduced without the
written consent of the publishers
Library of Congress Catalog Card Number: 66–24382
Made and printed in Great Britain by
William Clowes & Sons, Limited
London, Beccles and Colchester

Contents

Acknowledgment

The author and Publishers wish to thank those who have helped in the preparation of this book. The wallhanging *Moon* (104) is reproduced by kind permission of the Directors and Trustees of the Victoria and Albert Museum, London, and figures 44, 68, 73, 80, 98, 125, 126, 132, 133 and 134 have been specially taken by Tony Evans.

To my wife

Preface

This book is for readers who are interested to know how a tapestry is woven and for those who would like to weave a tapestry themselves. I have tried to write and illustrate it in such a way not only that the experienced weaver can understand but also that a beginner without any knowledge of weaving will be able to follow.

The craft of tapestry weaving is a very ancient one and the mechanical means employed have undergone little change. The methods are simple and direct. Weaving can be done without costly equipment and without much involved preparation. It gives an opportunity to use yarns whose colours and textures are different to those which are employed in any other media. It is a craft which grows slowly, one shape following another, one overlapping the other. Tapestry weaving is one of the few crafts which must be carried out by hand, and gives the craftsman an opportunity to produce something which the machine cannot.

The weaver is at the present time at a problematic stage. He can weave and design for the power-loom or weave something which the power-loom cannot weave economically or at all. Weavers hitherto have been weaving either utility fabrics or for luxury and decoration. Today the first group is unnecessary. The power-loom does the utility weaving—if not better (and this is an arguable point)—at least more quickly and cheaply. For the weaver it remains for him to weave for luxury, originality and beauty. Nothing can be more rewarding than the knowledge that one's work is desired not only for the sake of need but for its meritorious craftsmanship and aesthetic value. There is a growing demand for better design and colour which the craftsman must satisfy with products that are better than (or, at least, different from) those of the power-loom. With the growing demand for individually made things there are and will be more artist-craftsmen.

A new revival in tapestry started in France before the war and is carried on by studios and individual craftsmen in other countries. The reason for it is perhaps the reaction to mass production; to own, on the part of the collector, and to create something unique on the part of the artist.

Since Jean Lurçat reduced the number of colours, shades and spacing in the warp (from about 24 ends per inch to 12 ends per inch), tapestry weaving has undergone more simplifications and experiments. The time of producing a tapestry has been minimized and the method simplified. The design itself has changed. Abstract and geometrical forms are more easy to follow and more suitable for tapestry than the near naturalistic forms of the past. With the great changes in art, the craft of tapestry has been rediscovered. A new interest in the last fifty years in primitive art as well as in folk art with its tapestries as a by-product is another reason for the revival of tapestry. The Coptic and Peruvian weaving as well as folk weaving of Poland, Mexico, the Scandinavian and other countries is influencing the weaver more and more. He therefore finds a wider circle of people who are interested in and who are buying his work. Modern interiors of private houses and official buildings are very suitable for a hanging which gives warmth and colour to the very severe style in modern architecture.

As an encouragement to the would-be tapestry weavers I would like to abolish the fallacy that this craft is a very difficult one and that it takes years of practice to accomplish. It *does* require patience but it is a fascinating craft and the time required to learn it should not take more than for any other craft.

T.B.

Bromley, Kent 1966

What is a tapestry?

The word tapestry, which comes from the Greek τάπης and Latin *tapesium*, covers many different techniques. Tapestry was used in Greek and Roman times as a covering for furniture and floors, as well as for curtains and wall hangings, and was even used as a decorative feature in clothes. Tapestries have been embroidered, printed and painted as well as woven. Canvas work is sometimes even now called tapestry and the famous Bayeux Tapestry was embroidered in surface stitchery. Today tapestry is used mainly as a wall hanging and is almost always woven.

This book will deal only in woven tapestry, which is a weft surface fabric with a simple or complicated design. The weft threads are woven back and forth, through two alternate sheds and should be close enough together to cover the warp ends completely. The weft is woven in sections according to the pattern. It is a one sided fabric, as its main purpose is as a wall hanging where only one side is seen. The wrong side, which faces the wall, has all the ends of the weft left hanging. Only a very simply designed tapestry could be reversible with all the ends woven in as in Kelim, a rug technique, which is nearer to tapestry both in appearance and technique than any other form of weaving. (Kelim is used mainly as a floor covering; the weft and warp are of coarser yarns, hence the design is very simple.)

Woven tapestries can be divided into two groups, those woven on a vertical loom (high warp) and those woven on a horizontal loom (low warp). The vertical loom, roughly speaking, consists of two rollers supported by two uprights; the top roller is for the warp and the lower for the woven tapestry. The even numbered warp ends are separated from the uneven ones by means of a rod. The even numbered warp ends run on top of the rod leaving the uneven numbered warp ends under the rod. Every uneven numbered warp end is encircled by a leash (heddle) which is tied to a leash rod (heddle rod) (*16* and *17*).

The first shed is made by the rod (rod shed), the second by pulling the leashes (heddles), a few at a time, with the left hand towards the weaver, enabling the weft, wound on a bobbin, to be passed through the shed with the right hand. The weft is beaten down with the tip of the bobbin or a beater (comb) (*28* to *32*). The weaver works on the wrong side of the tapestry. Owing to the many different colours and shapes, the weft does not always pass from one selvedge to another without interruption, as in ordinary weaving, but is woven in sections according to the design. Each colour is wound on a separate bobbin, which, after use is left hanging on the back of the work until it is required again. There may be dozens of bobbins so hanging, and it would be a waste of time to search for the desired one on the other side of the loom. Each commencing and finishing weft yarn hangs loosely, cut to about one inch long, on the wrong side of the tapestry. Hence woven tapestry is one sided; it would take too long to finish off all the ends, besides being totally unnecessary. Only a very simple design could be worked on the right side.

A mirror placed on the other side of the loom will enable the weaver to see how his work progresses. In high warp weaving the cartoon is placed either behind the weaver or beside him. (I usually put the cartoon behind the warp (*29* and *30*).) It is helpful to trace the major outlines of the design onto the warp in order to keep the main proportions of the design.

Low-warp tapestry is woven on a horizontal foot loom. On this loom the warp is stretched from one roller, at the front, to a second roller, which is at the back of the loom. As in the upright loom the front roller is for the woven tapestry and the back roller for the warp. Every warp end passes through a heddle or heald. The heddles, through which the even numbered warp ends pass, are attached to one shaft and the heddles with the uneven numbered ends are attached to another shaft. Each shaft is tied to a pedal. The separation of the warp ends is made by pressing alternately on each pedal (*33* and *34*). Instead of a bobbin a flute or a flat shuttle is used and the beating down is done by a beater (or comb).

The cartoon on this loom is placed under the warp and is wound on to the front roller together with the woven tapestry. By placing the cartoon directly under the warp the original design can be copied exactly.

There is no visible difference between a tapestry woven on a high warp or on a low warp. Sometimes a red thread is inserted into the border of a high warp tapestry as a mark of identification. Weaving on a low warp loom is quicker than on a high warp loom, but the high warp gives the craftsman more freedom because it is more accessible and he can see more easily what he is weaving. In the case of a large tapestry more than one weaver is able to work on it. Low warp tapestries, if on a larger scale, can be woven in strips which are sewn together afterwards.

If the majority of lines and shapes are vertical, the tapestry is woven sideways, as it is easier to weave lines and shapes running across the warp than along the warp (*134* and *135*).

Linen, wool or cotton yarns are used for the warp; wool is usual for the weft, but silk and metal threads may also be used.

Today, many tapestry weavers use their own individual methods, yarns and equipment and adapt the technique to their own creative needs.

Historical background

We can only assume that tapestry weaving followed the invention of weaving or coincided with it. Tapestry weave was easier to produce on primitive looms than any other weave and the first weavers produced a coarse but very strong and even fabric. The creative desire for more pictorial representation inspired the invention of this craft as can be seen from the weaving of the primitive people of Borneo, Central Asia and Tibet, the Indians of America and the ancient inhabitants of Peru.

One of the first known tapestries was found in an Egyptian tomb of the period 1400 B.C., and one of the first written records mentioning tapestry weaving is by Ovid (43 B.C.–A.D. 18) in his *Metamorphoses* (VI 55–69) in the story of the competition between Minerva and Arachne. A great number of specimens of the second to fifth century made by Egypto-Roman craftsmen support the supposition that tapestry was woven in Ovid's time.

Another evidence of the early existence of the craft is examples now in the Hermitage Museum in Moscow. These were found in the tomb of the Seven Brothers at Temisiouck, formerly a Greek settlement in the province of Konvan on the north-eastern shore of the Black Sea. They are the work of Egyptian weavers from 1450 B.C. and Greek weavers in the third or fourth century B.C.

Further records of tapestry weaving are found in the Ben Hassan wall painting (1600 B.C.) which shows a weaver sitting on the ground and weaving on a horizontal loom (low warp). A Greek vase of the fifth century B.C. has a design which shows Penelope weaving a tapestry on a vertical loom (high warp); the warp is fastened to a top roller and each warp end is weighted down; the even-numbered warp ends are separated from the uneven ones by two cross sticks and the weft is beaten upwards.

Evidence of a high warp loom where the warp is taut and fastened to a top and lower roller is illustrated in the Codex of Rabamus Maurus (ninth century A.D.). From this we can see that the loom and the actual weaving of tapestry have not changed much up to the present day, the only main innovation being the leashes (heddles) which enabled the weaver to find the required shed more easily.

Artificers such as the Roman Plumarii, wove tapestries with figures of Britos (*Virgil*, 70–20 B.C., Georgics III, 25) *Purpurea intexti tollant Anlaca Britani*. Others had scenes from stories such as that of Theseus and Ariadne.

The sixth century A.D. mosaics of the Emperor Justinian and the Empress Theodora at Ravenna show numerous hangings as well as costumes decorated with tapestry, which indicate the fecundity of this period. From the fifth century A.D. and for many centuries later tapestry weaving was executed in monasteries, convents and castles under the patronage of the Church and courts.

The oldest western European tapestry in existence, woven in northern France or Germany, dates from the eleventh or twelfth century, and comes from the church of St Gereon, Cologne. During the Middle Ages tapestry weaving was carried out on a large scale in Flanders and in France. The Flemish weavers began to produce tapestries towards the end of the twelfth century and the French followed their example in the thirteenth century. Towns such as Arras, Valenciennes, Tournay, Oudenarde, Lille, Brussels and Bruges were the tapestry weaving centres for nearly three centuries. The Brussels weavers obtained the order from Pope Leo X for the reproduction in tapestry of the Raphael cartoons intended for the Sistine chapel in the Vatican. Numerous painters, including Van Eyck, Roger Van der Weyden, Thierry, Steuerbout and Hugo Van der Goes, were commissioned to submit cartoons for the Flemish weavers. The oldest French tapestry preserved today is the Apocalypse tapestry, woven at the end of the fourteenth century, which is now in the Museum at Angers. This tapestry was woven by a Parisian craftsman, Nicholas Bataille, after a cartoon by the painter Jean de Bruges. The high standard of his work indicates that the art of tapestry weaving was not in its infancy and this tapestry was not Nicholas Bataille's first production. The famous series of tapestries now in the Cluny Museum, known as *The Lady with the Unicorn*, is another outstanding example of French tapestry weaving from about 1509 and 1513. In 1539 Francis I established a factory of high-warp weaving in Fontainebleau. During the years 1662 and 1664 the production of tapestries was concentrated in three centres, Beauvais, Gobelins and Aubusson, and up to the time of the French Revolution these centres produced a great number of large tapestries, but later the standard fell into decline. In recent years there has been a revival of tapestry in France which is associated with Jean Lurçat, Gromaire and other contemporary painters. Although French studios are still producing most of the tapestries today, there are many individual artists, such as Eva Anttila in Finland, and small studios in Poland, Czechoslovakia and Portugal creating contemporary tapestries.

In Italy the princes of the house of Este invited two Flemish masters, Jean Mille and Raynel Grue, to Ferrara in 1564 to weave tapestries. Their successors, according to Vasari, executed a series of tapestries from the cartoons of Mantegna and Giulio Romano and Battista Dossi. Other ateliers were opened at Correggio in 1480 and another at Modena in 1488, but they did not last. In 1546 another tapestry-weaving atelier was opened in Florence. In 1632 there was an attempt to manufacture tapestries in Rome; a further attempt was made in 1702 and several tapestries after paintings by Carlo Maratti, Domenichino and Guido were woven there.

In Spain tapestries were woven after cartoons by Rubens, and Goya painted a considerable number of cartoons for tapestries which can be seen in the palace of the Escorial. In 1716, Peter the Great opened a workshop in Petrograd and in America William Baumgarten established the industry of tapestry production at Williamsbridge in New York City. The workshop was still active in 1918 under Foussadier, who went there from England after the closing down in 1887 of the Royal Windsor Tapestry Works which had existed since 1876.

In England, tapestry weaving is known to have been practised before the sixteenth century. Edward IV passed a law in 1344 for the regulation of the manufacture of tapestries. In 1399 the Earl of Arundel disposed, by will, of the hangings in his castle, which had been made in London of 'blue tapestry with red flowers'. In 1595 the monks of Canterbury were weaving tapestries for the Cathedral. About 1561 a tapestry weaving factory was established at Barcheston in Warwickshire by William Sheldon with the assistance of the master tapestry maker Robert Hicks. A new factory was set up in 1619 at Mortlake in Surrey by Francis Crane together with the master weaver Phillip de Maecht. Skilled *tapissiers* were brought over from Bruges and Oudenarde and fine tapestries were woven there such as those from Raphael's cartoons of the Acts of the Apostles. These cartoons were bought by Charles I on the advice of Rubens.

After the execution of Charles I, its principal patron, and with the death of Francis Crane in 1703, production at the Mortlake factory ceased. About 1758 there was a tapestry-weaving workshop opened in Soho, as well as others in Fulham and Lambeth.

A further attempt to revive tapestry weaving in England was made at the end of the seventeenth century, in Exeter, by some French refugees.

William Morris was responsible for the more recent revival of high-warp tapestry weaving at Merton Abbey in 1881 with the collaboration of Burne Jones and Walter Crane.

How to weave tapestry

Choice of loom

As tapestry weave is based on plain weave almost any loom suitable for plain weave could be used for tapestry weaving. The choice of a loom will largely depend on the individual weaver, his methods and the kind of tapestry he intends to produce; also on the space available and how much money he is prepared to spend.

Yarns for warp

The warp yarn must be very strong as it is under tension while weaving and holds the weight of the tapestry if the tapestry is hung warp downwards. It must also be fairly smooth to allow the weft to be packed very closely. The yarn should be elastic to recover from stretching while making a shed, especially when using leashes (heddles). It should also have a strong twist as a soft twisted yarn would easily fray. To pack the weft down use either the tip of the bobbin or beater. It is during this operation that the warp suffers most.

Cotton twine is the best warp yarn. Worsted spun thick yarn can be used, although it is very difficult to obtain.

Linen, I find, is more difficult to use, mainly because it is brittle and an unboiled linen yarn stains easily.

Colour is not the dominant factor when the warp is completely covered, but in the more experimental tapestry, where the warp shows occasionally and is part of the design, a coloured warp should be chosen accordingly. The majority of tapestries are woven on a white warp but a grey or beige coloured is more restful to the eyes if one weaves for long stretches at a time.

Yarns for weft

The weft makes the design. Each different yarn has its individual qualities and texture and, when packed very closely, gives a different appearance; a smooth hard twisted cotton will give a 'gooseflesh' impression; a smooth hard twisted woollen yarn will give more stress to the rib effect. Even the same colour looks different in individual yarns.

A soft spun yarn covers the warp ends much more easily, but a hard twisted yarn gives a certain stiffness and more body to the tapestry. The experienced tapestry weaver should use a variety of yarns, but for the beginner, at least for the first sampler, I would advise the use of one kind of yarn throughout, such as 3 ply or 2 ply knitting wool, crewel wool or tapestry wool, such as is used in embroidery.

The beginner will find it difficult at first to find the right yarns and colours. Besides crewel or tapestry wools which can easily be bought in small quantities, other yarns such as cheviot, saxony, botany and worsted can only be bought in larger quantities. It will take some time to make a collection of a wide range of colours and a variety of yarns. The other possibility is to buy white yarn and dye it. Each fibre, however, requires a different method of dyeing, and for this it is advisable to consult specialised books on the subject.

Spacing of the warp

The closeness of the warp depends on the design (or vice versa). The closer the warp the finer the weave and the smaller the shapes that can be woven. The weft threads will be thinner and the fabric itself will be finer and lighter accordingly. Tapestries have been woven as fine as 24 ends per inch and even closer. Such fine tapestries are very expensive but not necessarily better; on the contrary, the very fine warp has the tendency to give the weaver too much freedom in building up shapes so that the strong and bold design characteristic of tapestry disappears and the work tends to have the appearance of painting. Since Jean Lurçat reduced the number of warp ends to 12 per inch, tapestries are woven more quickly and cheaply and the design has gained in boldness.

I weave mostly on an 8 ends per inch warp and would recommend this to a beginner. A single warp end is strong enough for a small or a medium sized tapestry; a larger tapestry should have a double warp end.

High warp

The frame

For those not experienced in weaving, the high warp is the easiest with which to start. The frame is the basic apparatus: it is cheap to make or buy and does not require a great deal of space, and it is also easy and quick to set up the warp. The principle of its mechanism is probably the prototype not only of tapestry weaving but also of any kind of weaving. Some early illustrations show frame-like looms with the warp fastened to the top beam and the warp ends being kept taut by means of small weights, such as stones or clay, which were tied to each warp end individually or at the bottom of a group of ends. The weft instead of being beaten down was beaten upwards and the separation of alternate ends was made by finger manipulation. The Indians of old Mexico and other parts of America use frames as looms to this day.

Size of frame

This is determined by the size of the tapestry. To calculate the width of the frame add 2 in. to 3 in. to the width of the tapestry and the thickness of the wood used for the frame. The height of the frame should be the length of the tapestry plus about 25 in. and the thickness of the wood. The 25 in., measured from the top, is the wastage.

A tapestry can be woven up to about 23 in., measuring from the top; beyond this point weaving is more difficult because it is harder to get a large enough shed for passing the weft.

About 2 in. should be allowed for wastage from the lower part of the frame, more, if the tapestry is to be finished off with a fringe.

The thickness of the wood will depend on the size of the frame. For a frame about 2 ft × 4 ft, wood 2 in. × 1 in. should be strong enough. For larger frames the thickness should be increased accordingly. For a frame approximately 6 ft × 6 ft use 3 in. × 2 in.

A high grade wood of pine or poplar is recommended as it is easy to drive nails into these without cracking the wood and they can take a good deal of tension.

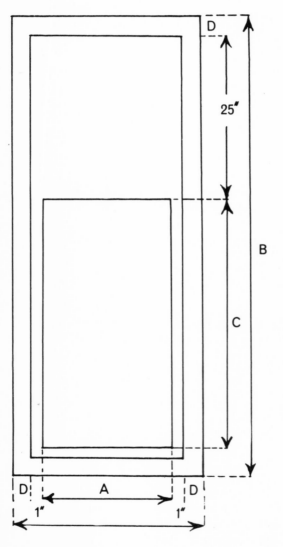

1   Making a frame
   A = *width of tapestry*   C = *length of tapestry*
   B = *overall length*   D = *thickness of wood*

Making a small frame

Frame I (2)

Size 2 ft × 4 ft for a small tapestry 18 in. × 23 in.

With two screws on each end join four pieces of wood measuring 1 in. × 2 in. × 24 in. to two uprights 1 in × 2 in. × 48 in. A should be screwed to the top of E and F, and B to the bottom of E and F; C and D to the other side of E and F alternately opposite to A and B. Put a block of wood (1 in. × 2 in. × 4 in.) centrally between the two top pieces (A and C) and the bottom ones (B and D). This is to prevent the wood bending under the strong tension of the warp. Mark inches on A and B starting 3 in. from the left side. Drive in rustless nails or screws on two levels (or more), two nails to the inch. If the nails are not on two levels the wood might split.

An additional nail should be driven in between the first and second nails on the left and right side top and bottom. This is to strengthen the selvedge and keep the warp ends closer on each side. The nails should be at an angle (*3*).

In addition to the frame, two cross sticks ($\frac{1}{4}$ in. × 1 in. × 2 ft or $\frac{1}{2}$ in. × 1 in. × 2 ft) are required; two rods, one rod to make a shed (about 1 in. to 2 in. in diameter × 20 in. or a rectangular piece of wood 2 in. × 2 in. × 20 in.); another rod for leashes (heddles) (1 in. in diameter × 26 in. long or a rectangular piece of wood 1 in. × 1 in. × 26 in). Two clamps to which the leash rod (heddle rod) will be fastened. Clamps are ideal for this purpose as the rod with the leashes (heddles) must be moved upwards while the weaving progresses.

Larger size frames must be made of thicker wood accordingly. A support of some kind should be made in each corner of the frame so that the frame will not warp. To avoid warping of the frame, while the warp is on, fix the frame to a wall or to any firm structure.

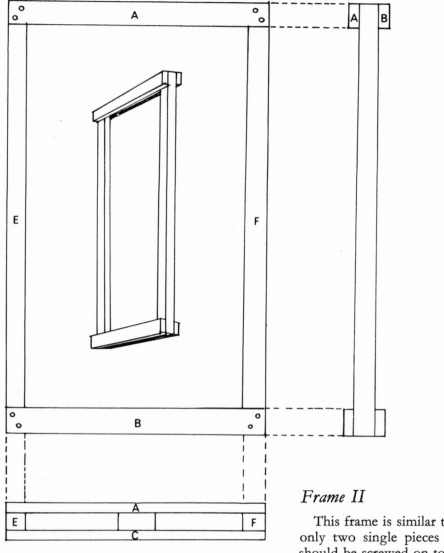

Frame II

This frame is similar to frame I except that only two single pieces of wood, A and B, should be screwed on to the two uprights, E and F. These two pieces A and B should be of a thicker wood ($1\frac{1}{2}$ in. × 2 in.).

There is no need for the shed rod, and only one cross stick is required.

2 *Frame I*

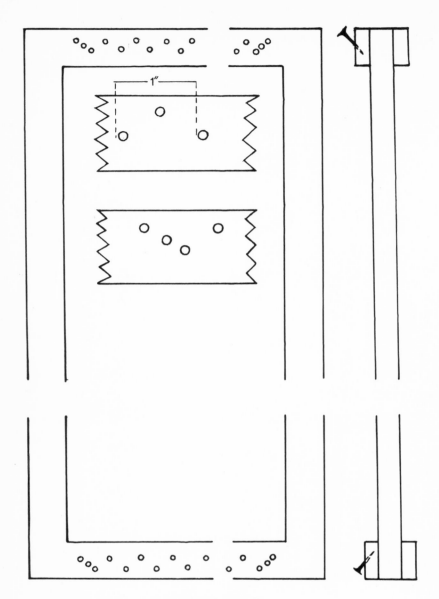

1"

3   *Frame I showing position and angle of nails*

Frame III (4)

This kind of frame is fitted with a tensioner to release and tighten the tension of the warp. The tensioner will enable the whole warp to be moved round. The advantage of this frame is that either a longer tapestry can be woven, or a smaller frame can be made but the main advantage is that the tapestry will always be on the same level because while the weaving progresses the whole warp with the woven tapestry can be moved round to the required level.

The calculation of the width of the frame is the same as for frame I; the length of the frame

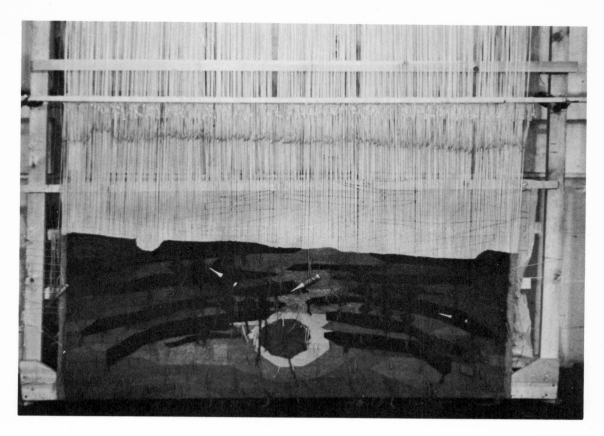

will be the length of the tapestry plus 48 in. divided by two. The 48 in. includes 25 in. wastage for shedding, 8 in. for the tensioner, 6 in. for tying on one side and another 6 in. on the other side, plus 3 in. thickness of the wood of the frame.

The tensioner consists of two pieces of wood 1 in. × 2 in. × 20 in. or 2 in. × 2 in. × 20 in. Drill two holes in each piece of wood, A and B, and insert two bolts, 10 in. to 12 in. long, with wing nuts. The holes on A must correspond with those on B (*5*). Make sure that the thread on the bolts is long enough; it should be 6 in. to 8 in. A larger tensioner is necessary for a larger frame; the length of the tensioner must be the measurement of the inside width of the frame. Three or more bolts should be fitted according to the length of the tensioner.

4 Frame III with a tensioner

5 A tensioner

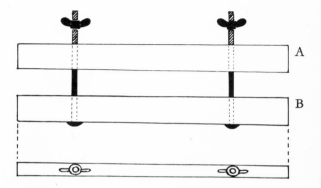

An additional two sticks, each $\frac{1}{2}$ in. $\times \frac{3}{4}$ in. $\times$ 20 in. long, should be added to the two cross sticks and the two rods. One end of the warp is wound round one stick and the other end of the warp is tied to the second stick (27).

An alternative method to the tensioner with bolts is to have two pieces of wood A and B to which the warp is tied direct, the two pieces of wood being tied together by strong string in several places at even intervals (6). To release the tension, release the strings and after moving the warp round, re-tie them.

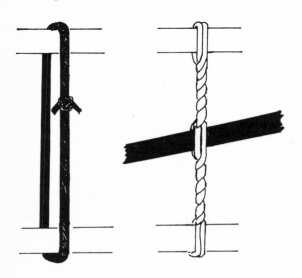

6 *Alternative tensioner*

Other types of frames

Although there are other different types of frames and the ways of putting on the warp differ one from another, the principle of weaving is the same. Some weavers make their frames to their own requirements and specifications. I, myself, make all my frames, in different sizes according to the size of tapestry to be woven, and I prefer to use frames to other looms.

Vertical foot loom

This loom has the advantage over the frame in that the separation of the warp ends is made by pressing down on pedals, which operate the shafts, similarly to the horizontal loom. Most of the vertical foot looms are designed for rug-weaving and have shafts the length of the width of the loom (inside measurements), which means that even if only a small shape has to be woven, instead of lifting a few warp ends at a time, all the warp ends must be pulled, one set back and the other forwards.

A vertical foot loom with sectional shafts is an ideal tapestry loom.

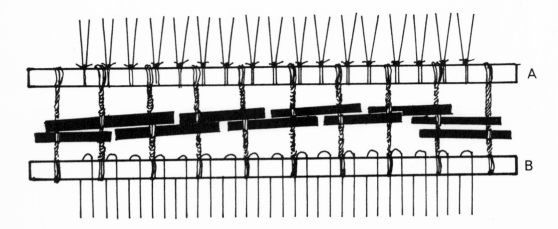

A

B

Setting up frame I

If a larger frame is used, prop it sideways on the floor against a wall. Stools or chairs could be placed under the frame.

Tie a thread with a slip knot (7) to the first nail on top of the frame on the left side, then take the thread, holding it tightly round the first nail on the right hand side of the frame and return again to the first nail on the left side. In this way we have the selvedge consisting of two warp ends. When the selvedge is finished, take the warp end to the second nail on the opposite side, go round it, and carry it to the second nail on the other side and so on, down to the middle of the frame, always keeping the thread under tension. When arriving at the middle of the frame, tie the thread temporarily, going round the next nail several times. Turn the frame upside down and continue warping upwards until the last nail is reached. From this last nail return to the last nail on the opposite side for the selvedge and fasten the warp end. Return the frame to the vertical position. (Figs *8* to *11* show several spacings of the warp.)

7 *Slip knot*

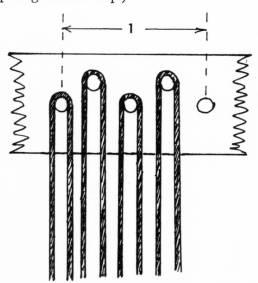

8 *4 nails per inch*
   8 warp ends per inch

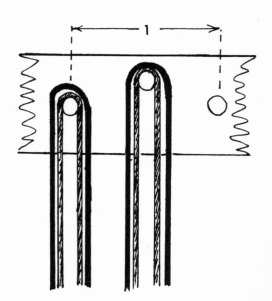

9 *2 nails per inch*
   8 warp ends per inch

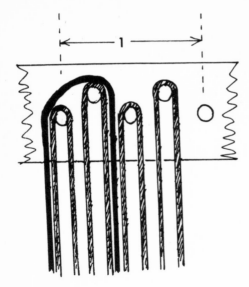

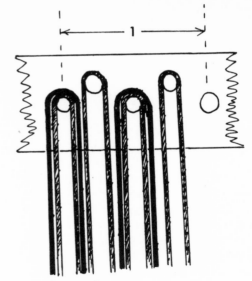

10 *4 nails per inch*
     10 warp ends per inch

11 *4 nails per inch*
     12 warp ends per inch

Correcting the tension

The warp should be evenly taut, but if it is slack in some places the tension should now be corrected. Usually the warp is tighter on the side where the warping ends than on the side where it starts. To correct the tension start from the tighter side towards the slacker by pulling on each consecutive warp end, on the side of each nail nearest to the slacker side, to the last nail. The warp ends will then be some inches longer. Undo the temporary knot and re-tie. The length of the 'left over' threads will depend on how tightly the warp is put on in the first place. If the warp ends are excessively long before the last nail is reached, cut off the surplus length and tie the ends together nearest to the nail on top of the frame, that is the side where the wastage for shedding will be. Make sure the tension is correct, as good tension is of great importance to a successful tapestry.

Setting up a very large frame

Place a box under each corner of the frame, wind the warp as described above only walk to and fro inside the frame, starting as before on the left side of the frame and taking the threads from the first nail on one side of the frame to the opposite first nail on the other side.

Inserting the cross sticks

When the tension is satisfactory, separate one set of the warp from the other by a rod 1 in. or 1½ in. in diameter and about 4 in. longer than the width of the warp. Instead of a rod a stick 1 in. × 1 in. or 1½ in. × 1½ in. can be used. In place of the rod or stick a provisional cross stick, 1 in. × ¼ in. thick can be used and replaced afterwards with the rod or the thicker stick.

Start with the first two single ends, that is the selvedge, put them on the rod, leaving the second warp end under the rod; put the third end on top of the rod, fourth under, fifth over and so on, thus leaving the uneven numbered ends on top of the rod and the even ones underneath. In order to avoid crossing the warp ends remember to have one thread on each side of the nail, and to pick the first one and put it over the rod. The next step is to secure the rod so that it will not slide off. Tie a thread on each side of the rod and tie the other end of the thread round the top of the frame. After securing the rod put the even numbered warp ends on top of a flat stick, about 1 in. × ¼ in. and longer than the width of the warp by about 4 in., leaving the uneven numbered ends under it, which means the other threads from the other side of the nails. Selecting and separating the even from the uneven numbered warp ends is made easier if it is done nearer to the top nails, or nearer to the lower nails in case of a larger frame.

Tying leashes (heddles)

Method I

Cut 8 ply cotton, or a similar yarn, for leashes, 15 in. long, as many as there are even numbered warp ends. Encircle each even numbered end with the prepared cotton. When 4 even numbered ends are encircled, tie the 4 leashes together with an overhead knot leaving them about 2 in. to 3 in. long measuring from the loop to the knot (*12* and *13*). This method is practised only if a simple design and a small frame are used.

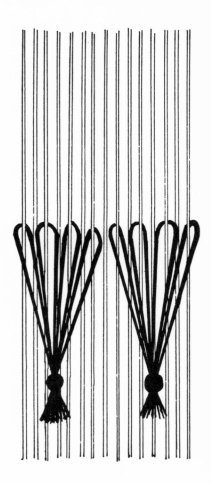

12   Tying leashes, method I

Method II

A much better way, instead of tying leashes (heddles) into fours, is to tie them each individually onto a rod. This is a method which is widely applied in high-warp weaving and all the high-warp weaving in France is based on this method, the great advantage of it being that any number of leashes can be

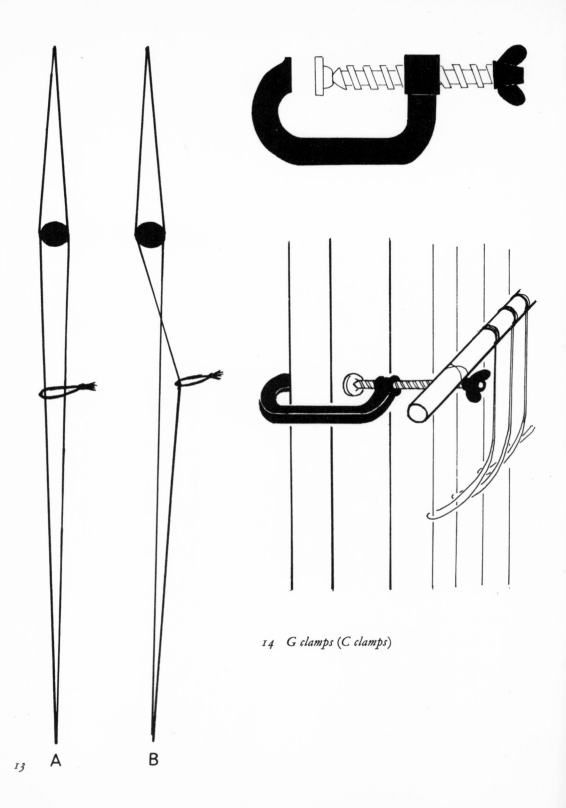

13   A   B

14   *G clamps (C clamps)*

selected and it is easier to find them, as they are attached to a rod. In the previous method the leashes (heddles) tend to slide down.

A rod 1 in. or 1½ in. in diameter, about 2 in. longer than the width of the frame, should be tied to a clamp on each side. The G clamps (C clamps), about 9 in. long, should be fixed on each upright side of the frame and about two-thirds from the bottom (*14*). The idea of the clamps is that one can easily move the rod higher while the weaving is progressing. Any other device similar to the clamps could be used.

For leashes (heddles), which should be tied to the rod, cut the cotton about 20 in. long. In order to keep all the leashes the same length push the cross sticks down, about 12 in. below the rod, to which the leashes (heddles) will be tied. Secure the cross sticks by tying them to the two uprights of the frame. Encircle each warp end which runs under the top cross stick and over the bottom one, with a leash (heddle), which should be tied to the leash rod (heddle rod) (*15, 16, 17*).

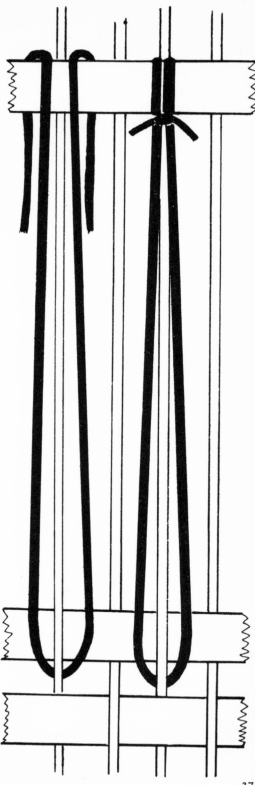

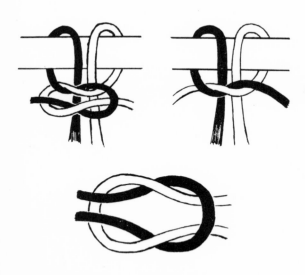

15 *Reef knot used for tying leashes*   *16*

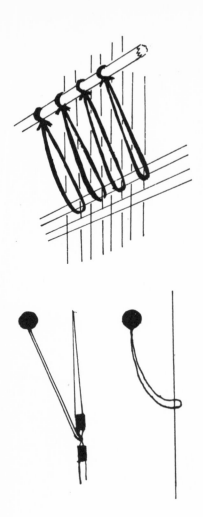

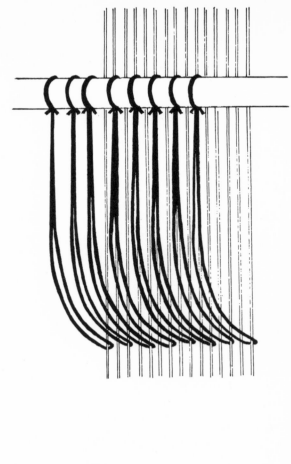

16

Method III

Instead of having leashes (heddles) tied in fours and hanging loosely or tied onto a rod on the weaver's side, that is on the front of the frame, the leashes (heddles) can be tied in a manner similar to the inkle loom principle, to a stick which is fixed on the back of the frame. The advantage of this method is that it is easier and quicker to pass the weft both ways, from left to right and from right to left, from one selvedge to another or in sections, having both hands free while passing the weft.

This method I find has more advantages than the previous one when big shapes are woven but it is less suitable for very small areas of weaving.

The warp should be put on in the same way as previously described. Turn the frame with the warp side towards a wall. Tie a piece of wood 1 in. × 1 in. × the width of the frame plus 1 in. to 2 in., in the middle and across the frame, to each upright. Place the cross sticks, which are separating the warp ends, on the same level as the stick on the back.

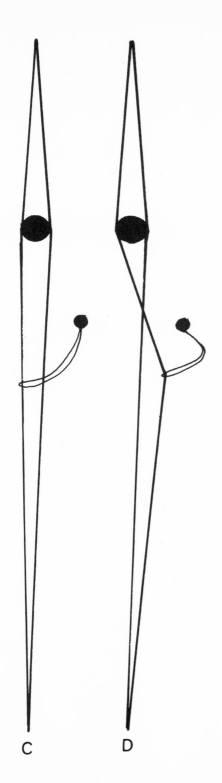

Cut some string for leashes (heddles), about 20 in. to 30 in. long. Tie the beginning of the string firmly on to the left side of the stick, opposite the selvedge of the warp, take it round the first warp end, which runs under the top cross stick and over the bottom cross stick, bring it back to the stick, take it round the stick twice, crossing the string in order to keep it firmly in place, and encircle the next warp end which runs under the top cross stick, repeating this until only a few inches of the string is left. Cut a similar length and tie it to the last string and continue as before until the last warp end on the right side (*18*). It is easier to make the leashes (heddles) a few inches at a time, as a longer string for leashes (heddles) tangles more easily. Avoid knots next to the warp ends; always keep them at the back of the stick. The distance between the warp and the stick should be about 2 in. and all the

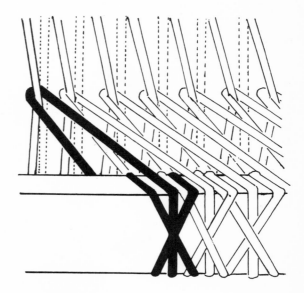

18 Method III

17 Method II

C   D

leashes (heddles) should be as nearly as possible of the same length. Unevenness in the
length of the leashes will result in an uneven
shed. Stick a piece of adhesive tape right across
the back of the stick where all the leashes
(heddles) cross each other, to prevent the
leashes (heddles) moving about and thus
changing their lengths.

A more organized method is to prepare the
leashes beforehand, cutting them to 6 in. to
8 in. long and making loops at each end (*19*).
Mark inches on the back of the stick and drive
in nails every ½ in. Hook one loop of the leash
(heddle) onto the nail, go over the stick and
round the warp end which runs under the top
cross stick, take it back and under the stick
and hook the second loop onto the same nail.
Hook the next leash onto the same nail, which
means there will always be 2 leashes hooked
on each nail (*20*). When all the warp ends are
encircled, turn the frame so that the warp is
facing the weaver and the stick with leashes is
on the back. Turn the top cross stick on its
side and pass a piece of wood (shed stick)
1 in. × 2 in. × the width of the inside of the
frame, through the opening. Push the top
cross stick as high as possible and secure it
with string. The reason for keeping the top
cross stick is that if the shed stick should fall
out it is very easy to find the shed again. Push
the bottom cross stick right down the warp.
By moving the top piece of wood (shed stick)
either up or down we obtain 2 alternative
sheds. When the shed stick is pushed right
down on the leashes, all the uneven numbered
warp ends which are encircled by leashes
(heddles) will be in front, leaving the even
numbered warp ends behind the shed stick,
thus creating one shed (*21A*). When the shed
stick is pushed upwards the even numbered
ends will come forwards and the uneven ones
will stay behind about 1 in. to 1½ in. (*21B*).

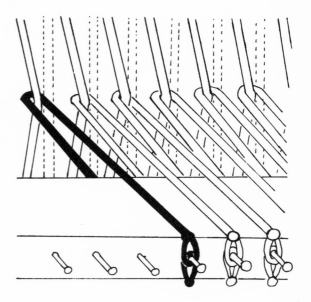

20

The difference between this method and the
previous one is that in the former the free
warp ends remain stationary and only the encircled ones with leashes (heddles) move
backwards and forwards, in this the opposite
happens: the free warp ends move backwards
and forwards and the encircled ones remain
stationary.

If the shed stick is pushed upwards and the
shed is not big enough, put a block of wood
between each upright of the frame and the
leash stick (lease stick) (*22A* and *23*). The
depth of the shed will depend on the thickness
of the block.

If the other shed is too small, that is when
we push the shed stick down, the shed stick
should be replaced by a thicker one. The size
of this shed is the thickness of the shed stick
(*22B*).

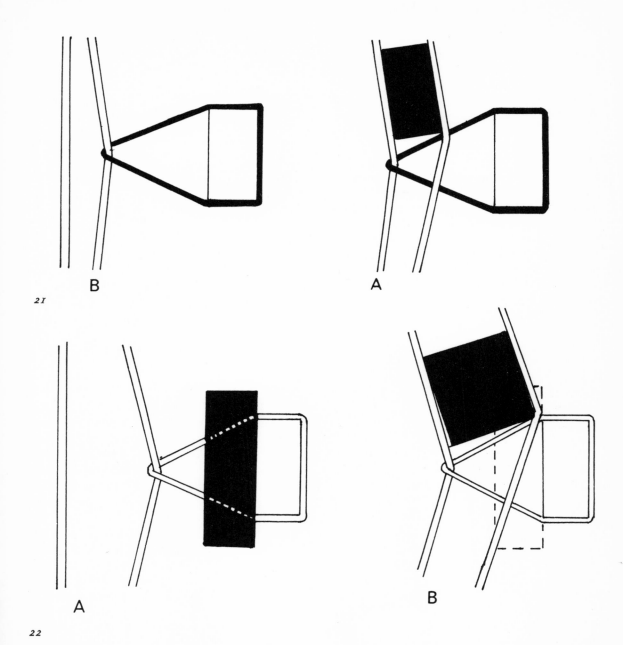

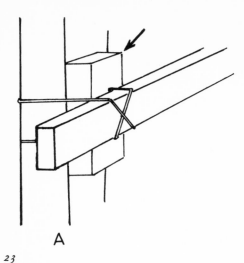

A

23

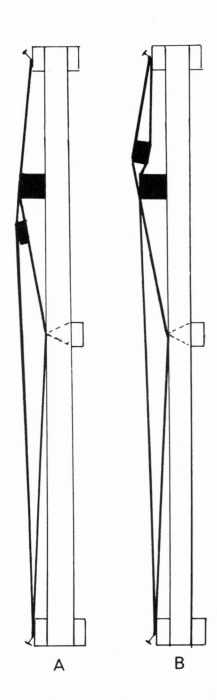

24

When weaving in small sections, that is when weaving smaller shapes, where there is no need to go with the weft right across the warp from one selvedge to another for a long stretch, a short shed stick can be used. Push the long shed stick as high as possible and insert a shorter one under it. A boat shuttle is very useful for this job. Sometimes the shed stick, when pushed upwards, slides down of its own accord. To prevent this either put another stick under the warp, about 15 in. from the top, thus tightening the tension of the warp which will grip the shed stick (if the shed stick still slides down, push it above the other stick (24)) or tie a length of string to each side of the shed stick, fling them over the frame and weight them down. This way one can even manipulate the shedding (25).

Setting up frame II

Using a G clamp (C clamp), clamp the frame longways and on its side on top of a table, in such a way that half of the frame projects outwards. Tie the cotton thread provisionally at the middle of the left side, carry it over and

A   B

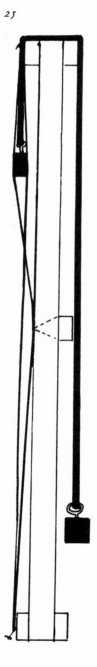

under the right side, take it back under and over the left side. Repeat this taking the warp thread round and round the frame until the required width is reached. Tie the thread and reverse the frame. Then proceed in the same way as before, starting from the middle. Correcting the tension and putting on the leashes is similar to frame I. The only difference is that there is no need for a shed rod as the shed is created by the thickness of the wood, and the leashes encircle the warp ends which are behind the frame (*26A, B*). If a small frame is used put two nails, or screws, in the middle on the outside of each upright. Put the frame between two stools or chairs so that it pivots on the nails and the frame can be turned round and round while putting on the warp (*26E*). Another method is to wind the warp in a figure of eight movement, so that the warp ends cross each other in the middle (*26C, D*).

Setting up frame III

Tie the tensioner provisionally to stick A and to stick B (*27*); then tie both sticks together, taking the cord round the frame. On a small frame the warp ends could be cut individually. Loop them round stick B and tie to stick A in groups of eight or more warp ends. Tie the warp to the back stick A as it is easier to correct the tension while weaving. Use a reef knot as shown in fig. *15*. Tie the warp once (*15*), correct the tension until it is perfect, then complete the knot (*15*). A longer warp should be prepared either on warping posts or a warping frame (see page 43). Making leashes (heddles) is similar as for frame I. Commence weaving above stick B. To turn the warp round release the tension by unscrewing the bolts on the tensioner. (It is better to turn the warp round when the weaving is being carried out more or less on the same level.) While turning never pull on

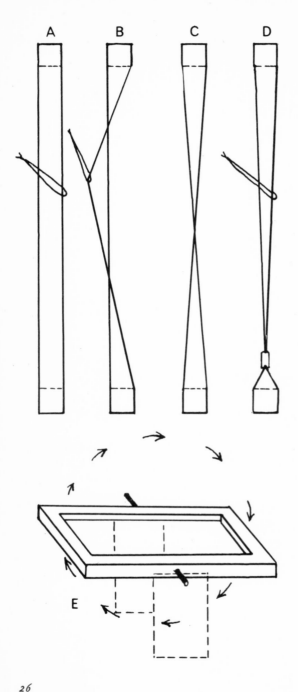

the individual warp ends, only pull down stick B (and push up stick A). Instead of the tensioner the alternate method can be used (6). Before undoing the cords to release the tension, provisionally tie very loosely both sticks A and B. Then undo all the cords. Turn the warp round and tie the cords again. To get a tighter tension use sticks as shown in fig. 6 and twist them.

Weaving on a frame

Before starting to weave, wind some wool on a bobbin. Wind the wool as tightly as possible and if several threads are being used together keep an even tension on all of them. Wind the wool slightly diagonally, and then reverse it on the other side (28). It is better not to wind too much wool at a time as it will only unwind and the threads will tangle. Anyhow wind only a little at a time on the bobbin as the beginning of the sampler will be an exercise not only to find out how to weave but to discover what thickness of the weft yarn should be used. Therefore wind, for the first ½ in. of weaving, only 1 thread of 2 or 3 ply knitting wool or 4 threads of 2/24s or 2/25s worsted. If any other yarns are used, the thickness should be about the same as for the wool or worsted.

On a frame with leashes (heddles) (methods 1 and 2) it is better to weave using the rod shed to take the weft from right to left and using the leash shed (heddle shed) to pass the weft from left to right. One should keep to this method whenever possible. Sometimes it is necessary to pass the weft through using both sheds either way.

Starting with the rod shed (this shed is always open due to the thickness of the rod), take the weft from the right side to the left. Hold the bobbin, with the weft, in the right hand between the thumb and first finger in a

26

34

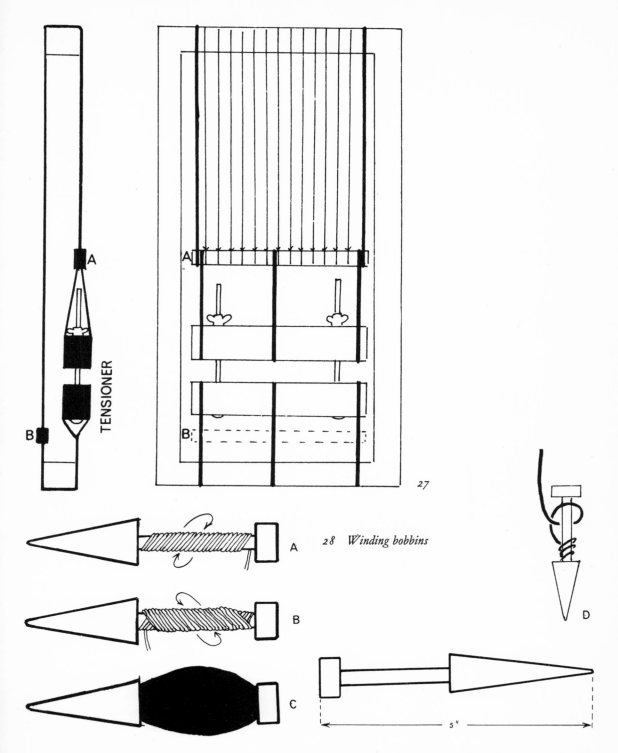

TENSIONER

27

28 *Winding bobbins*

A

B

C

D

5"

35

Passing the weft from right to left   *A*   *B*

vertical position. Put the four fingers of the left hand through the shed from left to right, starting on the right side of the warp, always weaving in small sections of about 2 in. to 3 in., widen the shed slightly by turning your four fingers horizontally and make a small gap

between the first and second finger; pass the bobbin with the right hand through the shed from the right side to the left, holding the bobbin vertically, and putting it between the first and second finger of the left hand. Close the fingers on the bobbin and withdraw the

C   D

left hand with the bobbin, which should always be in a vertical position whenever passing through a shed. Repeat this until the left side is reached (*29*). Always weave in small sections of 2 in. to 3 in., which could be increased later on. Do not pull the weft too tightly;

always leave a small semicircular loop, which should be as symmetrical as possible, and beat down the weft with the point of the bobbin (*30* and *32*). When beating down, the loose end of the weft should be held with the other hand.

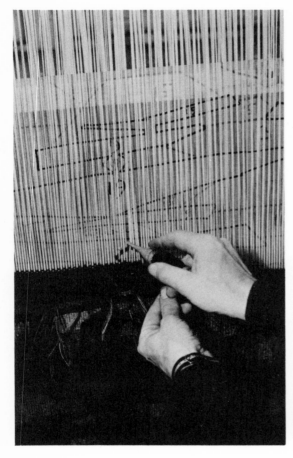

31 Passing the weft from left to right A

In order to fasten off the beginning of the weft, take it around the selvedge, divide the selvedge, and put the end through the same shed.

To pass the weft from the left to the right side pull the 4 leashes (heddles) tied together,

or in the case of leashes (heddles) attached to a rod, pull the first 4 to 6 leashes (heddles) at a time, towards you with the left hand, thus creating a shed. Hold the bobbin in the right hand between the thumb and first finger, as before. Pass the other three fingers of the right

B

C

hand through the shed from the right side to the left, roll the bobbin vertically from the left to the right side through the shed (*31*). It is a good idea to practise this with an empty bobbin before starting to weave. Pass the weft, from the left side to the selvedge on the right side. Weave again in 1 in. to 2 in. sections, leaving a semicircular loop and forcing it down with the bobbin, while holding the loose end in the other hand (*30* and *32*).

It is very important to leave the semicircular loop. If the weft is too tight, not only

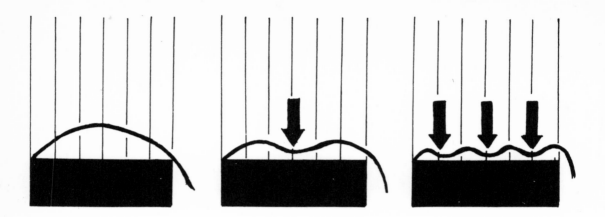

32

will there be difficulty in covering the warp but the width of the tapestry will tend to go in. On the other hand, if too much weft is allowed, small loops will be created.

Special care must be taken of the selvedge. Take the weft once more round the selvedge on each side, after 2 or 3 picks, when changing the shed and passing the weft through the shed, pull the weft tightly and beat down the weft around the selvedge. From there again leave a small loop, which should be forced down. This is to make the selvedge taut and firm. Another method of keeping the selvedge firm is to pull the selvedge ends and the 2 or 3 first ends on each side very close together. This will keep the weft very firm.

After weaving some picks the weft should cover the warp completely. If there is any difficulty in covering the warp leave the semi-circular loop slightly bigger.

After weaving about half an inch and using

1 thread of 2 or 3 ply knitting wool, wind 2 threads, or if using 2/24s or 2/25s worsted wind 6 threads onto the bobbin. Weave about ½ in. to 1 in. The thickness could still be increased later on. It will soon be apparent whether the weft thread is too thick or not. If too thick a yarn is used it will be difficult to cover the warp. A too thin yarn has the tendency to pull in the weaving. After finding the right weft thickness use it throughout the sampler.

To join a fresh weft yarn, leave the last end of about 1½ in. long hanging and start with the fresh weft next to the last one, leaving the end of the fresh weft hanging about 1½ in. as before. There is no need to overlap the weft as tapestry weave is very firm and when packing the weft very closely both the ends will stay firmly in the web. Only in a very loosely woven tapestry should one overlap the new one for about 1 in. over the old weft yarn.

Low warp

Horizontal foot loom

Low warp is woven on a horizontal foot loom, which basically consists of two strongly built sides which stand on the floor in an upright position; joined to the two sides are two rollers, one at the back, the other at the front, two rest beams and other beams holding the loom rigidly together. The warp is stretched from the back roller, on which it is wound, to the front roller. The rollers are fitted with a ratchet wheel which controls the tension and the winding or unwinding of the warp. The opening of the sheds is made by means of heddles. The even warp ends pass through one set of heddles which are attached to one shaft and the uneven ones pass through another set of heddles which in turn are attached to the second shaft. The two shafts are tied alternately to pedals which when pressed, one at a time, lift one shaft up and lower the other and vice versa, thus making a shed (*33* and *34*). For tapestry weaving only two shafts are necessary, but four shafts

can be used as well. If there are four shafts on a loom, the shafts are connected first to the lams, which in turn are connected to the pedals. Foot looms have either overslung or underslung battens (beaters) to which a reed is attached. For tapestry weaving the reed is mainly used for the spacing of the warp; only in rare cases is the reed used for beating down the weft. Therefore the problem of which loom is more suitable, with an over- or underslung batten (beater), is not very important.

I am writing about the foot loom in very general terms as there are many books dealing with it, and concentrating only on adapting it to tapestry weaving.

Preparing the warp

In order to make a longer warp, warping posts, a warping frame or a mill is necessary. Warping posts are only suitable for shorter warps, up to 3 yards long, a frame can wind up to 7 yards or more and mills up to 32 yards.

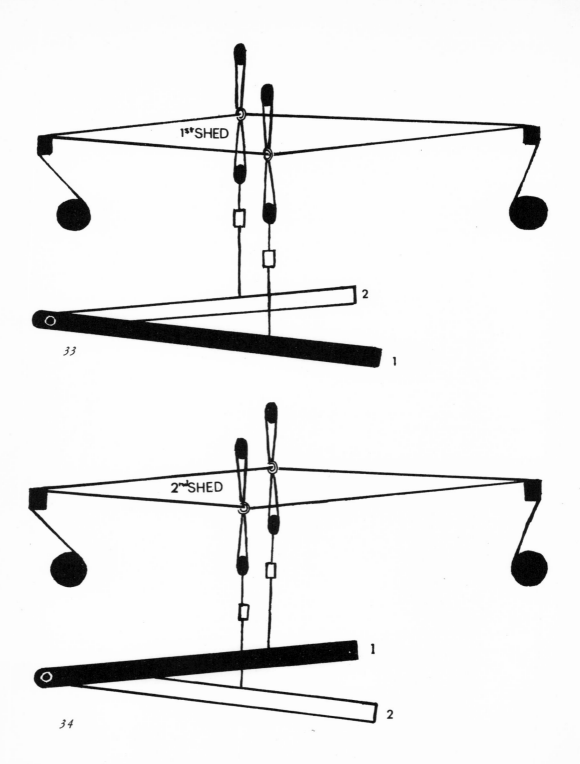

1ˢᵗ SHED

33

2

1

2ⁿᵈ SHED

34

1

2

42

Warping posts

The warping posts consist of a block with
three pegs, which should be secured by means
of a clamp to one end of a table and another
block with only one peg, which should be
fastened on the other side of the table (*35* and
36). The distance from one block to another
should give the length of the warp.

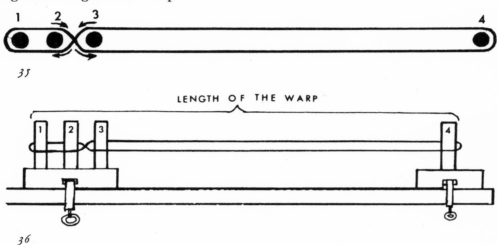

35

36

Warping frame

The warping frame is basically similar with
three pegs on one side and another one at the
end, other pegs being added to make the
required length (*37*).

37

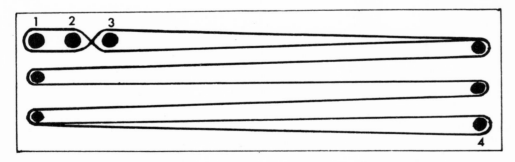

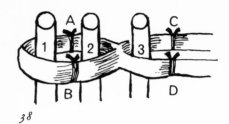

38

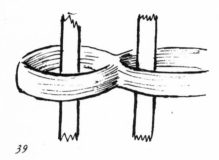

39

Warping mill

The warping mill works on the same principle only the warp is wound round the mill to the required length.

Length of the warp

The length of the warp is the length of the intended tapestry plus about 30 in. to 40 in. for wastage.

Width of the warp

The width of the warp is the width of the intended tapestry plus 1 in. to 2 in. for 'going in' plus selvedge. If 8 single ends per inch, add only 2 more threads to the total, or add 4 more if 8 double ends, for the selvedge.

If 8 ends per inch, take either a single thread or 2 threads at a time. It is simpler for the beginner to take a single thread at a time, but it is quicker to wind using two. If 2 threads are used they must be counted as 2, 4, 6 ends and so on. Tie the threads to the first peg, go over the second and under the third, round the last peg and return. Returning, go over the third and under the second and first peg; and again over the first and second and under the third and to the last peg. The warp ends will cross each other between the second and third pegs. Repeat this until the required number of warp ends is completed. Secure the cross in four places A, B, C and D, nearest to the second and third peg and at E, nearest to the last peg (38), or put one cross stick between A and B, on one side of the cross, nearest to the second peg, and another stick between C and D, nearest to the third peg. Tie the two cross sticks together, on each side, leaving about 2 in. to 3 in. space between them (39). Take the warp off from the last peg, chain it and take it off completely from the warping posts, frame or mill (40).

The next step is to space the warp through a reed. If a 4 dents per inch reed is used, put 2

44

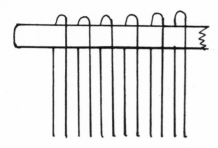

40

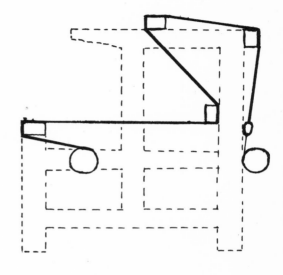

41

ends through each dent. When there are 4 ends in every loop cut them so that 2 ends will be threaded at a time through each dent and then tied together afterwards. In both cases a stick must be passed through each loop. If an 8 dents per inch reed is used, cut the loops of the warp and thread one end through each dent, tie them together again and put a stick through the loops. Tie the stick with the warp to the roller in front of the loom and wind on some warp leaving only enough for threading through the heddles. If only two shafts are used thread 2, 1, 2, 1 ... *ad lib*, putting 2 ends through the first and last heddle for the selvedge if single threads are used, or 4 ends if double ends are used. On a four shaft loom thread 4, 2, 3, 1. After threading through the heddles, wind the warp from the front roller and tie at the back. If a longer warp is used put one or several beams on top of the loom (*41* and *42*).

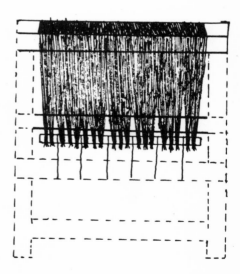

42

For a very long warp the conventional way of beaming must be used.

When only two shafts are in use tie them each separately to a pedal. In the case of four shafts and if the threading was 4, 2, 3, 1, the fourth and third shafts should be tied to one pedal and the second and first shafts to the other. Shafts 1 and 2 could be tied together, and so could 3 and 4, as they are going to be lifted at the same time.

Weaving is similar to that on a frame. Flat or roller shuttles can be used to wind the weft and pass it through the shed. An empty bobbin is necessary for beating down the weft.

Press one pedal, pass the weft through the shed, finish off the end by taking it round the selvedge, divide the selvedge and put it through the same shed. Leave a big semi-circular loop, divide it into 2 or 3 loops by beating it down with the empty bobbin. Sub-divide the loops again and again into 2 in. to 3 in. ones.

For the beginning of the tapestry and when the weft is woven from one selvedge to another, the reed could be used for beating down. Otherwise a bobbin or a beater (comb) should be used. The reed also could be used for forcing down the weft of a very simple tapestry if the different coloured weft threads are laid on the same level. If the reed *is* used, make the semicircular loops first and then beat down the weft with the reed in the same shed, that is the open shed.

Weaving shapes is the same as described for the frame (page 47), the only difference being in the manipulation of the sheds.

As the weaving progresses, release first the ratchet on the front roller, then on the back roller, release a few inches of the warp and tighten it up with the front roller. If the tension of the warp has to be corrected in separate sections, undo the section, which is tied to the back roller, correct it and re-tie.

Weaving a sampler

Before weaving a small tapestry it is advisable to weave a sampler first. Even a narrow sampler (about 4 in. wide) would help in overcoming the first difficulties and would acquaint the weaver with different techniques.

The sampler could be woven either on an upright or on a horizontal loom. If possible, the first sections of the sampler should be woven on one set of warp set up on a frame, and the other sections on a horizontal loom. This way, one not only experiences the difference but also finds out which loom suits the weaver better. Different methods of setting up the frame or foot loom could be applied while weaving the sampler. For the first sections use the same type and thickness of yarn in the weft but towards the end of the sampler it is interesting to experiment with different yarns of various thickness and texture.

In the sampler illustrated, the spacing is 8 ends per inch but 10, 12 or even finer spacing can be used. The warp is 32/24s cotton twine. The weft is 2/24s worsted, 6 threads plyed together; the colours are black and white. The length of the sampler is about 40 in., therefore the length of the warp is (40 in. + 25 in. for the wastage = 65 in.). On a small frame two or three lengths must be woven, one after the other, in order to weave all the sections.

First section Weave about 1 in. or 2 in. in depth, using one colour (black in the sampler illustrated). This is to practise covering the warp and to keep the width straight.

Second section The second section would consist of two colours, black and white, therefore use two bobbins or flat shuttles (if weaving on a horizontal loom). Weave 1 pick, that is 1 row, using black thread and after changing the shed weave the white thread for the second pick. Repeat these 2 picks for about 2 in. The black thread will cover only the even numbered warp ends and the white the uneven ones, giving vertical lines (*43A, 44*).

When weaving pick and pick, one pick of one colour and the next pick of another colour, cross one colour over (or under) the other so that they lock, otherwise the selvedge will be missed out (*45*). Fig. *46* shows how to avoid showing the crossing of threads on the

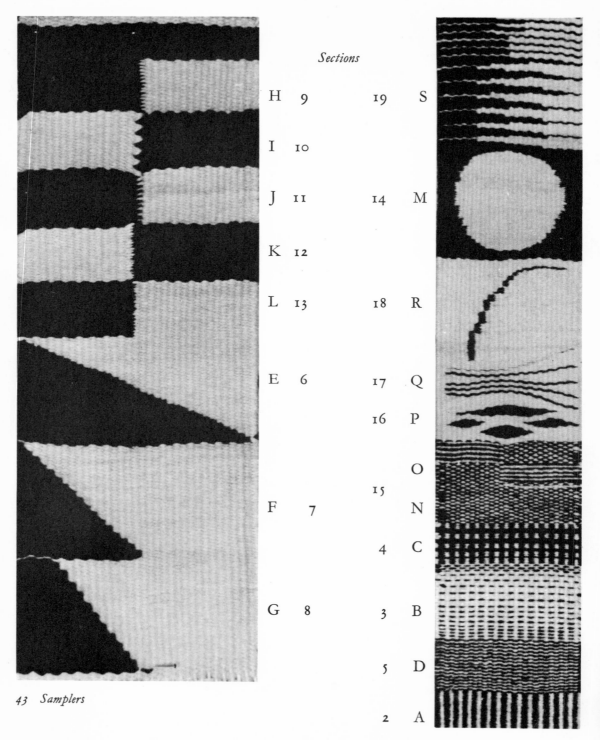

Sections

H 9 19 S

I 10

J 11 14 M

K 12

L 13 18 R

E 6 17 Q

16 P

O

15

F 7 N

4 C

G 8 3 B

5 D

43 Samplers

2 A

44 'Two Islands Meet' approximately 6' × 6', orange, red and purple on deep green background showing the use of pick and pick in the middle of the tapestry. Cotton warp

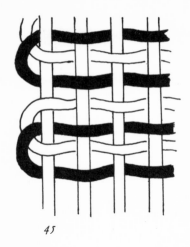

45

Fourth section For the fourth section weave pick and pick, 1 pick of black and 1 of white for about ¼ in. and then weave 3 picks of black. After this weave again pick and pick for another ¼ in. and then weave 6 picks of black and so on increasing the amount of the black picks. This will give white squares; if reversed, that is weaving white instead of black, for several picks, this will give black squares (*43C*).

Fifth section Weave 2 picks of black and 2 of white. This gives slightly wavy lines going across the warp (*43D*). To avoid loops on each side of the selvedge, cover the black with the white and vice versa on the other side. This applies in all cases when the loops, on the selvedge, should be covered (*48*).

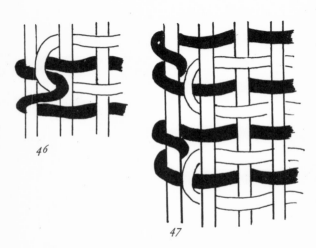

46

47

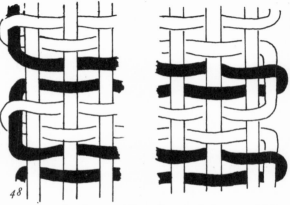

48

selvedge. Pull the loop onto the wrong side. Another way is to miss out the last two warp ends on each side, either with the black or white thread (*47*).

Third section Weave 3 picks of white and 1 pick of black for about ½ in. Then 5 picks of white and 1 of black for another ½ in. and 7 picks of white and 1 of black. This will result in gradual shading by widening the gaps between each black pick. If an even number of white picks is woven between each black pick, the black will not appear in the same line; it will be staggered (*43B*).

Sixth section Start with a diagonal shape which is the basic shape in tapestry. Weave with the black thread from the first warp end on the left side of the sampler and take it to the last warp end on the right side. Change the shed and return the weft to the second warp end on the right side. Change the shed and pass the weft from the second end to the last one on the left side. From there, after changing the shed to number 3, from 3 to the last and so on, missing one warp end on the right side (*43E* and *49*). When weaving the diagonal shape and leaving one warp end at a time, it is very easy to miss two warp ends instead of one. This is because of the shedding. The weft finishes

50

once on the left side of a warp end and then on the right side of the adjoining warp end. Therefore every other time, when the weft

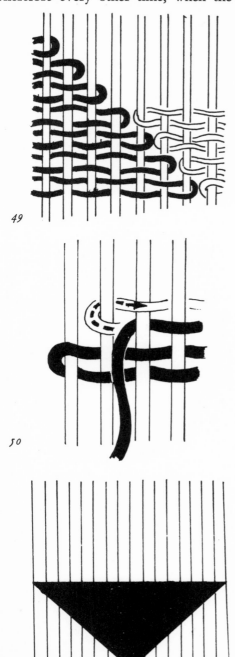

49

50

51

finishes on the right side, take the weft round the warp end (*50*). After completing about 2 in. in black, weave the background, that is the white. Start from the first warp end on the right, take the weft round it, then carry it round the second, third, fourth and so on, building up the shape in steps, adding one warp end, each time, on the left side. There is no need to join the two colours as the slits are only minimal. It is easier and quicker to weave first one shape to a certain distance before weaving the adjoining area, or one can weave 2 or 4 picks with one colour at a time and then with the other colour. The shape which slopes inward must be woven first, otherwise the shed would become locked (*51*).

Seventh section To increase the angle weave 4 picks before stepping the weft to the left side. Start from the first warp end and take it round the last end on the left, return, and carry it round the second end on the right, back to the left selvedge and once more back to the second end on the right, round it, and back to the right selvedge. Then take the weft twice round the third warp end and twice round the fourth, fifth and so on weaving four picks before stepping to the next warp end. After 2 in. weave the white background. In this way the angle of the shape should be twice as steep as in the previous section (*43F* and *53*).

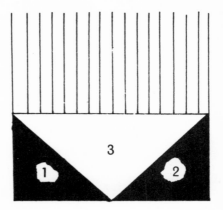

Eighth section To increase the angle even more, weave 6 picks before stepping to the next warp end (*43G* and *54*). By either increasing or decreasing the number of picks before making a step, different angles can be created (*55*). The steeper the angle, the longer are the slits. If the slits are longer than $\frac{1}{4}$ in. they should be sewn together afterwards or woven together while the weaving progresses.

The following sections will show how to join two colours vertically.

Ninth section Vertical dovetail (*43H*) Both colours go round the same common warp end (*56*). Start with the black thread from the left selvedge, take it round the middle warp end and return. Then carry the white from the right selvedge around the same middle warp end and return to the right selvedge. This method tends to 'build up' (*56C*). One can weave it up to about $\frac{1}{2}$ in. but it is very useful when weaving steep diagonal shapes (*57*).

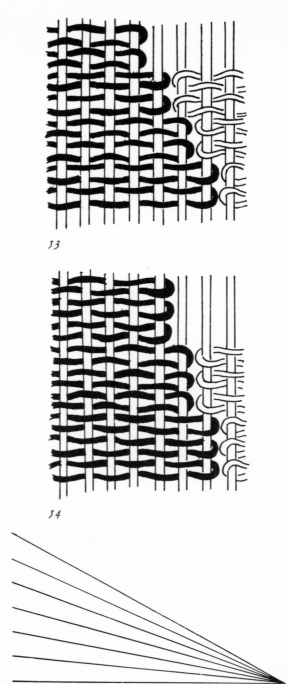

53

54

52   Detail from a small tapestry showing the use of simple shapes at different angles. Cotton warp

55

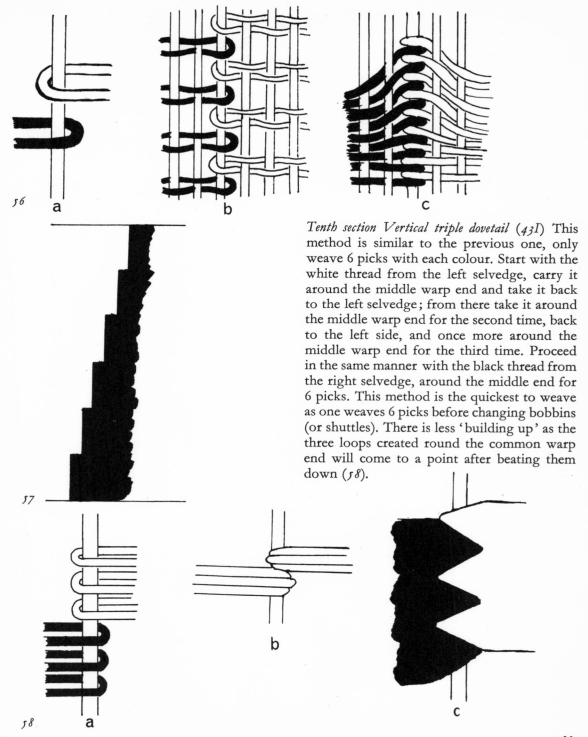

56 a   b   c

Tenth section Vertical triple dovetail (431) This method is similar to the previous one, only weave 6 picks with each colour. Start with the white thread from the left selvedge, carry it around the middle warp end and take it back to the left selvedge; from there take it around the middle warp end for the second time, back to the left side, and once more around the middle warp end for the third time. Proceed in the same manner with the black thread from the right selvedge, around the middle end for 6 picks. This method is the quickest to weave as one weaves 6 picks before changing bobbins (or shuttles). There is less 'building up' as the three loops created round the common warp end will come to a point after beating them down (*58*).

57

58 a   b   c

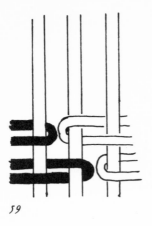

59

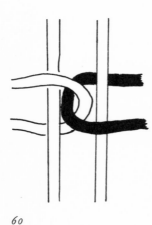

60

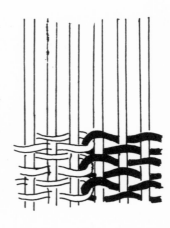

Eleventh section Vertical 3 warp ends join This method works on 3 warp ends and it is the strongest one (*43J* and *59*), especially if the tapestry is a large one and is intended to hang sideways. Start with the black thread, take it round the second warp end, chosen from the 3 middle ends, and return to the left selvedge. From there carry it to the first end (of the 3 warp ends) and return to the left selvedge. Then take the other colour from the right selvedge around the third warp end, return to the right selvedge and carry it around the second end, returning again to

the right selvedge. There is no tendency to 'build up'.

Twelfth section Vertical locked weft This method gives the clearest division of two colours, but it is more difficult and it is slower to weave (*43K* and *60*). Weave the white thread from the left selvedge, bring it to the middle warp end and leave it there. Bring the black from the right selvedge to the same point as the white one, cross it over and under the white thread; return the black thread to the right side and the white to the left.

54

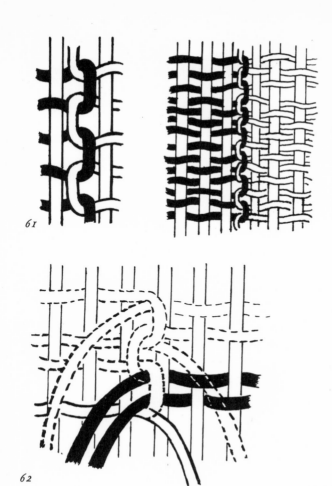

61

62

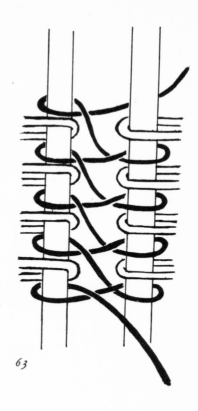

63

Thirteenth section Vertical interlocked wefts (43L and 61). Weave the black thread from left to right and leave it in the middle of the sampler. Start the white thread from the same point, leaving the end on the left side of the black thread. Take the white thread to the right and return to the same starting point, leaving the thread on the left side of the black thread. Then carry the black thread around the white threads to the left selvedge and bring it back to the middle point, leaving the thread on the right side of the white thread. After this take the white thread over the black threads, carry it to the right selvedge and bring it back to the middle (*62*). This lock is very strong and gives a clear division of two colours.

When wide areas (about 3 in. to 4 in. or more) have to be joined together, each strip can be woven separately, leaving slits on each side. The slits must be sewn together afterwards. In Kelims and some Gothic and Renaissance tapestries, all or some of the slits have been left unsewn forming outlines of, for example, a nose, mouth or chin. All the vertical areas must be woven perfectly straight. The slits should be sewn together on the back of the tapestry either on the loom, or better still after the tapestry is cut from the loom. For sewing use a half rounded upholstery needle and a strong thin thread, preferably a silk thread. The sewing should be invisible on the right side of the tapestry. Fig. *63* shows the method I use.

To join two colours a binder can be used, that is a very thin thread, running across, either from selvedge to selvedge or in sections (*64*). Weave 2, 4 or 6 picks at a time with the pattern making thread and then run the thin thread across for 1 or 2 picks. If a thin thread is used it should be invisible, but if a thicker binder is used it could be incorporated in the design.

65

64

On a horizontal loom two colours can be joined by bringing the two opposite colours together, locking them and taking them back to their own sides while in the same shed (*65*). Because there are two picks in one shed, the weft thread must be accordingly thinner. This way of joining two colours is rather limited and it can only be used in certain designs.

Fourteenth section Weaving a circle It is very difficult to weave a perfect circle and it is therefore better to design a polygonal shape (*43M, 66* to *69*). The method of weaving a circle is derived from a combination of diagonal shapes and joining two colours vertically. Draw the outline of the circle, with a marker, on the warp, or on a piece of paper which should be placed behind the warp. Start weaving the background on one side until the weft will go 4 times round the last warp and then weave the same on the other side. Two separate bobbins, or shuttles, should be used for the background, that is the white thread; one on the left side, the other on the right side. Weave the lower part of the circle with the black thread, until it would be on the same level as the background. From this point, join the black thread with the white threads on each side, using either the vertical dovetail or any other method of joining two colours vertically. Weave the shape following the outlines of the circle increasing the steepness (at first) and then decreasing it after the middle of the circle. If the circle is to be woven without joining, only to be sewn afterwards, weave first the background to the middle of the circle on one side, then weave on the other side. After this weave the circle, completing it and then weave the rest of the background on each side (*43M, 70* and *71*).

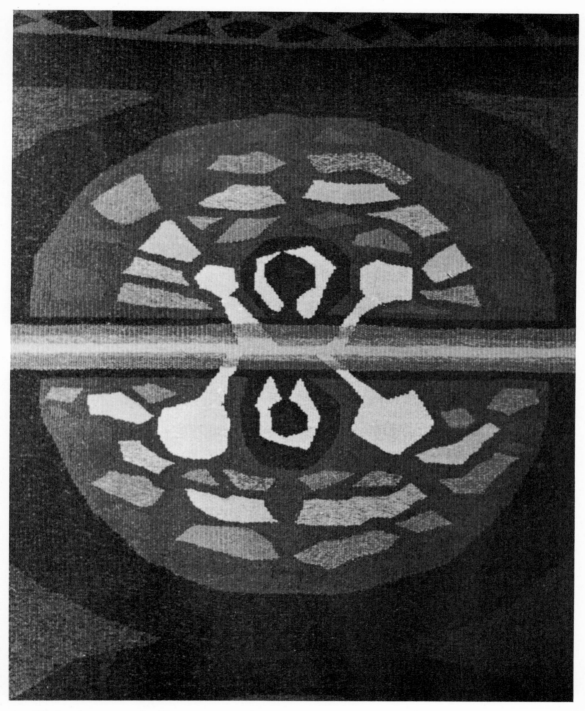

66 'Embryo' *an example of how to weave a circle-like shape. Cotton warp*

67 'Delta' a combination of worsted and cheviot yarns with a very fine spun jute showing the method of joining two colours vertically (see fig. 64). Cotton warp

68 'Red Moonlight'   *mostly reds. Cotton warp*
69 *Detail*

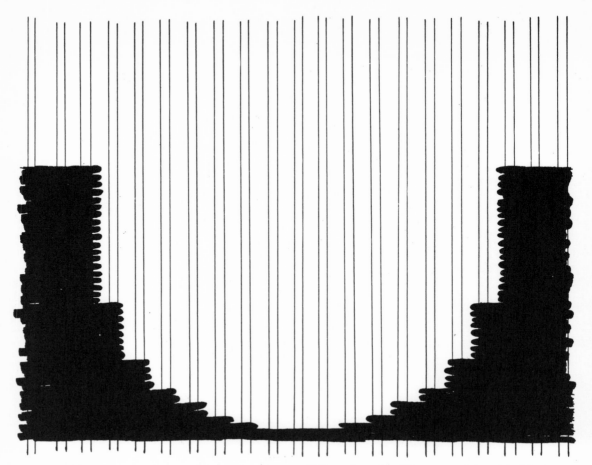

70

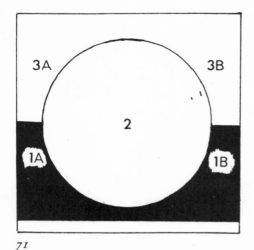

71

Fifteenth section Weave 1 pick with black and another with white but put both colours through the same shed. After passing the black, beat it down and then pass the white thread, without changing the shed. Only when both colours have been passed, change the shed and repeat as before (*43N*). By changing the order halfway through or at any point, a pattern can be made. Where the two white picks and the black picks meet, horizontal lines will be created (*43O*). Start as before, with black and follow it with white. In the next shed, instead of weaving first with black commence with white, carry it to the middle of the sampler and leave it there; then weave the black right across, and after beating down the black weft, place the white over the black. In the next shed weave with black again which should be followed by white. After this shed carry the white thread to the middle and leave it there; then weave the black right across and place the white thread over the black (72).

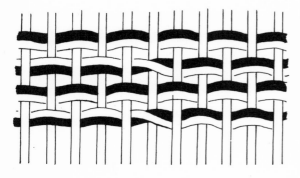

72

Sixteenth section The building up of shapes must be made in such a way that the shed is not locked. The only time when the shapes are woven outwards is in weaving spots and lozenges (43P, 73, 74 and 75). Weave the spots with black and then weave the white right across, without building up. The spots and lozenges can be of any width but their heights must not be exaggerated as it would result in puckering.

Seventeenth section (43Q) In this section build up a curved shape with the white thread; then weave 2 picks of black right across. Build up the background again and weave the lines in black. The background must always be woven horizontally, otherwise it will pucker. The angle of the shape should not be too steep (no more than 45°). Thick diagonal and curved lines should be woven horizontally, only thin diagonal lines (up to 4 to 6 picks) can be woven across (76 to 80).

Eighteenth section The thinnest vertical line is the width of one warp end. If the spacing is 8 ends per inch, the thickness of the line is 1/8 in., if 10 ends per inch, 1/10 in. and so on. The weft cannot simply be taken round and round a warp end, it must be joined on one side and sewn on the other side afterwards. To join the line use the vertical interlocked wefts method (page 55). Thin vertical lines should be avoided in tapestry but if there is need for such lines they should not be too close to each other as they will weaken the structure of the fabric. Curving the vertical line is made in steps (43R).

Nineteenth section (43S) Hatchings were commonly used in Gothic and Renaissance tapestries and by weaving elongated triangular shapes across the warp, shading and halftones are made. Special care must be taken not to weave both colours through the same shed (Figs 87 and 88).

These exercises show only the basic elements of tapestry weaving. By varying the texture and thickness of weft yarns and by changing the structure of the warp (varying spacing or thicknesses in the same tapestry) different results are obtained.

General notes

After weaving the sampler it is advisable to weave at least one small tapestry without any prepared cartoon. Of course there should be some general idea as to colour and shape, but the details should be worked out on the loom. After finding out what is possible and what is not, a more elaborate design can be worked out, and a cartoon prepared.

Place the cartoon behind the warp or draw the outlines on the warp with a marker.

On an upright loom fix the cartoon on to a stick, with drawing pins, and tie the stick to the two uprights and behind the warp.

On a horizontal loom the cartoon can be placed under the warp, pinned to the bottom of the selvedge using either pins or safety pins, and then rolled together with the woven tapestry.

73 'Winter' black and white on a grey background.
Use of lozenges (see page 61). Tapestry woven
sideways. Cotton warp
74 Opposite: Detail

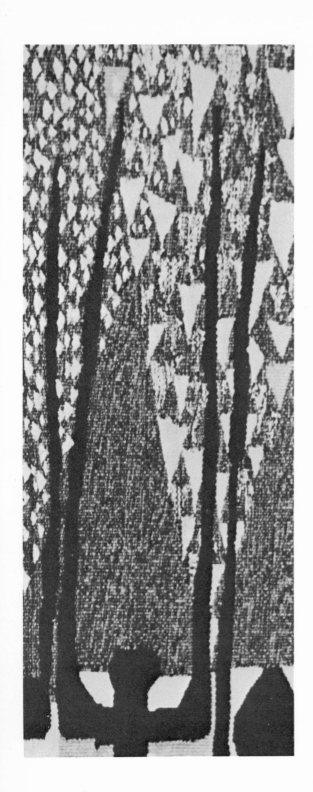

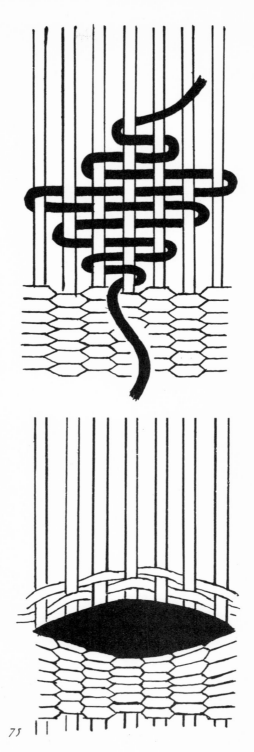

75

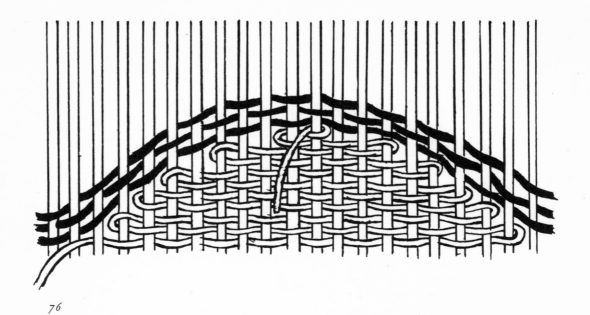

76

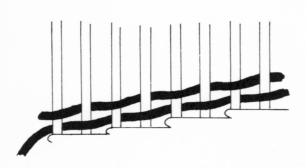

77

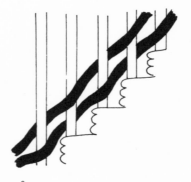

78

Weave a border of 3 in. to 4 in. at the beginning and towards the end of the tapestry for folding under.

When building up shapes do not weave them too high; no higher than about 5 in. above the other shapes.

Always weave the shapes which are going inwards first, then the ones going outwards. Fig. *81* shows a detail of a cartoon (*82*) for *Twin Constellation* (*83* and *84*) and the order in which the shapes should be woven.

It is important to commence with the subsequent colour on top of the previous one in such a way that the new thread passes through the next shed and no double thickness occurs in the same shed. Double thickness in the weft would result in the warp showing (*85* and *86*). In Fig. *85* the white thread (1) finishes in a different shed to the black one (2). The following black pick (3) therefore passes through the same shed as the white one (1). To avoid this either add another pick of the white thread or undo the last pick so that the white will finish

79   'Bird'   showing the use of novelty yarns and wavy
     lines. Tapestry woven sideways. Cotton warp

*80 Detail from 'Pollination' 4 ft 6 in. × 4 ft 6 in.,
red on black. Wavy lines have been used. Linen
warp*

in the same shed as the black thread; or skip the warp ends for the width of the white pick, and when returning the black, run through the next shed to the white one (*87*).

Fig. *86* shows a similar problem. The black thread starts from the right side, that is away from the white. This is wrong as it will result in a double thickness over the next step. Fig. *88* shows the right way. The black starts from the left side, that is running towards the white.

Another way is to run a thread on top and across the inward going shape, provided the angle of the shape is very low.

One of the main difficulties in weaving a tapestry is keeping an even width, and it is advisable to measure the width roughly inch by inch.

When leaving longer slits sew them provisionally using big stitches with a strong and contrasting coloured thread.

Watch that the warp ends are always straight; curving is due to bad tension either in the warp or weft

When the bobbins are not in immediate use, loop them and let them hang. Do not poke them through the warp.

When using a beater try to beat down evenly over the whole width of the tapestry. Do not concentrate just in one place.

All shapes should be woven slightly higher than on the cartoon as they will be pressed down by the subsequent picks.

66

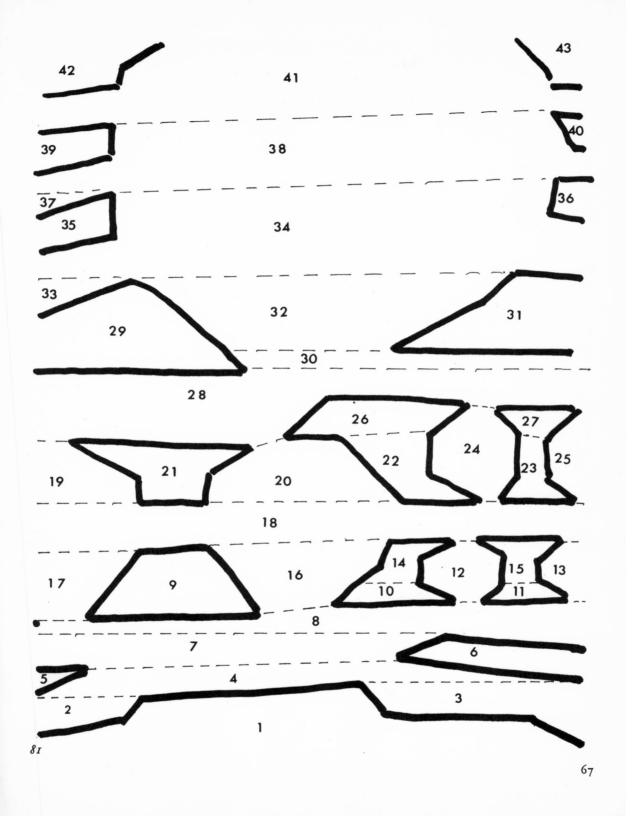

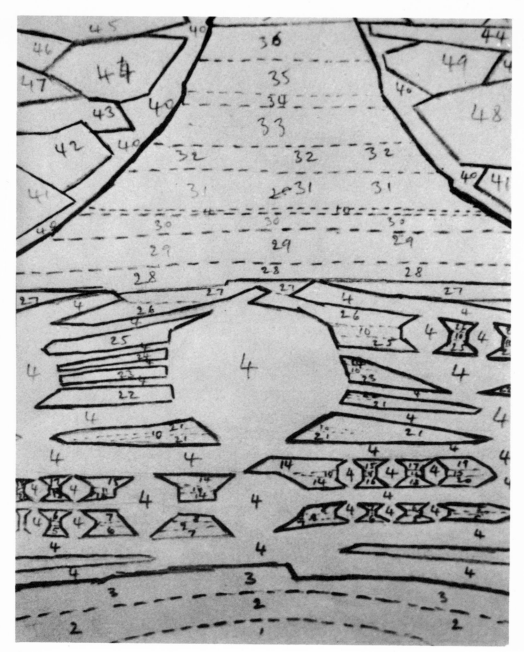

82

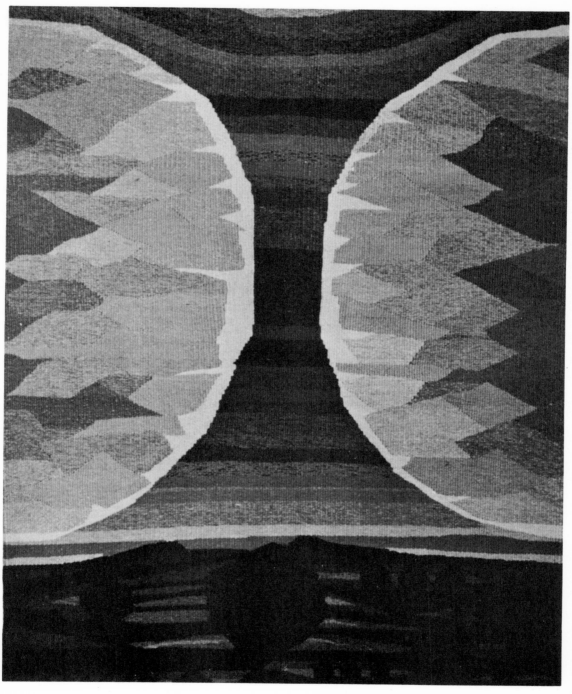

83 'Twin Constellation' a range of light and dark
reds. Cotton warp

84 Detail of 83

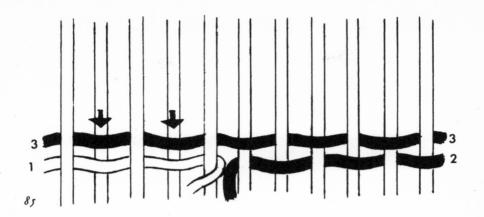

3   3

1   2

85

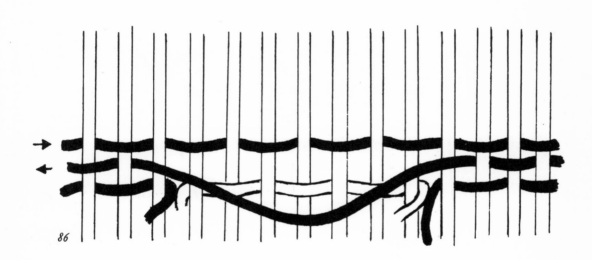

86

71

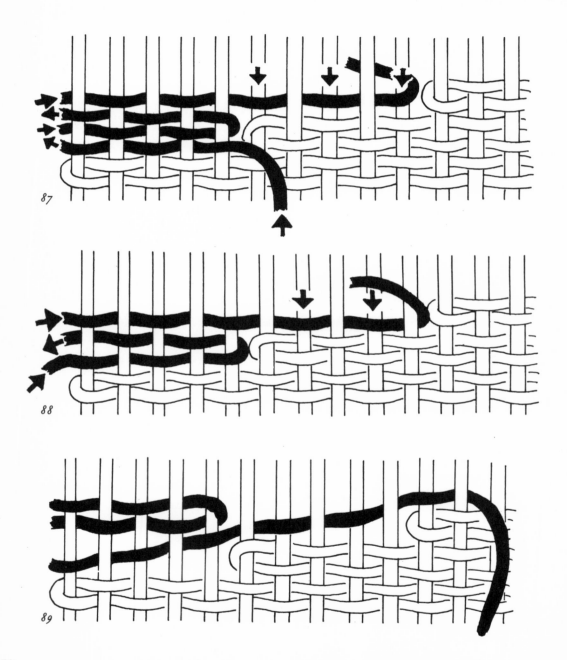

87

88

89

90   *91*

Special care must be taken of the width when weaving the last few inches. It is at this point that the tapestry is drawn in often due to hurrying. Wide shapes tend to go in more, therefore they should be woven slightly looser than the small shapes.

When the tapestry is complete, cut the warp about ½ in. close to the weave. Leave more if the tapestry is to be finished off with a fringe (*90*).

It is advisable to hemstitch the edge before the tapestry is cut off. Turn both ends of the tapestry under and stitch the edge in such a way that the thread (use a very strong thread, preferably silk), is invisible on the right side. Then sew a cotton tape along the edge. If the tapestry is to hang warp downwards a small pocket should be left in which to insert a rod (*91*). If the tapestry is to hang sideways sew some brass rings at even intervals (2 in. to 4 in.) on the edge from which the tapestry will hang. The rings should, of course, be large enough to let a rod pass through.

It is not always necessary to press a tapestry but if it has to be pressed, use either a steam iron or place a damp cloth under the iron on the wrong side of the tapestry.

How to keep an even width

The width of the tapestry is controlled by the tension of the weft. If not enough weft is allowed to go round the warp ends, the width will curve. If too much weft is allowed, not only are loops created but the fabric will widen. Uneven tension in the warp might also contribute to this. Another reason is that because tapestry is woven in sections, and the shapes are being woven in different parts, the beating down is uneven. Furthermore mixed yarns of different properties make an even width very difficult to maintain. There is no reed, unlike in ordinary weaving, to keep the width and even spacing of the warp. A reed could be placed either in the upper part of the frame to keep the spacing of the warp or on a horizontal foot loom in front of the shafts, but there is still some distance between it and the web. Even if the reed is used for forcing down each pick, the tapestry weave has so many more picks per inch, which makes the weft strength more dominant than in ordinary weaving. Only in small and simple tapestries can one use tenterhooks or temples which are used for ordinary cloth to keep an even width. But even then they would cover part of the weaving and it would be difficult to follow the design.

The best method, when weaving on a frame, is to loop short lengths of strong cotton, the same as used in the warp, round the edge, on each side of the woven tapestry which then should be tied to each upright of the frame (92). First weave about 2 in., thread the cotton with a needle through the edge, on each side of the tapestry, loop it round the uprights and tie with a slip knot. Weave 1 in. to 2 in. and repeat this again, only loop the thread about $\frac{1}{2}$ in. to either side from the previous point. Do not always use the same point as this will result in uneven spacing of the warp.

A similar adjustment can be arranged on a horizontal loom. Tie two sticks on each side of the loom to which then tie the short lengths of cotton.

It is advisable to measure the width after weaving practically every inch. The 'going in' process happens very gradually and is often only noticed when it is too late. The only remedy if the width curves in too much is to

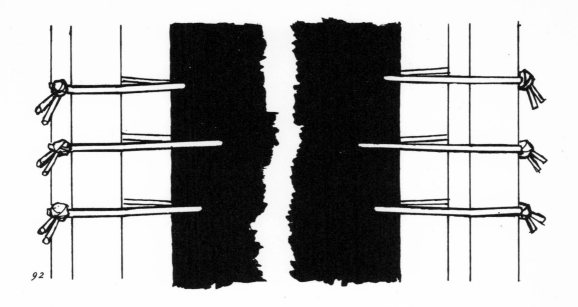

92

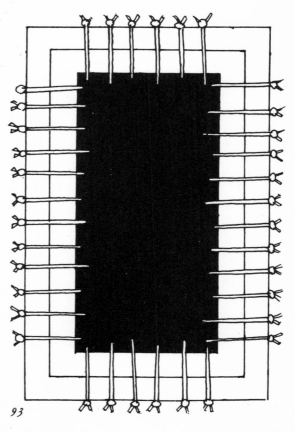

undo the work and start again. When the tapestry is finished and if the width is still uneven, stretch the 'going in' part and shrink the wider part by damping the whole tapestry and stretching it on a frame by a similar method as described above (93), or by pressing on the wrong side, with either a steam iron or with a damp cloth under the iron, those parts which need shrinking.

93

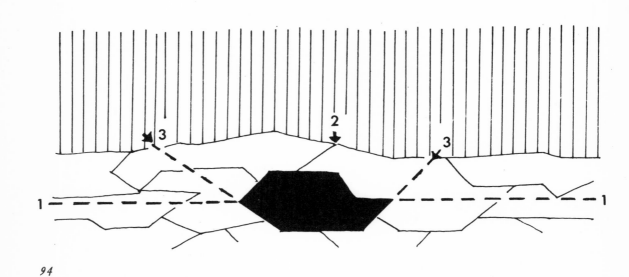

94

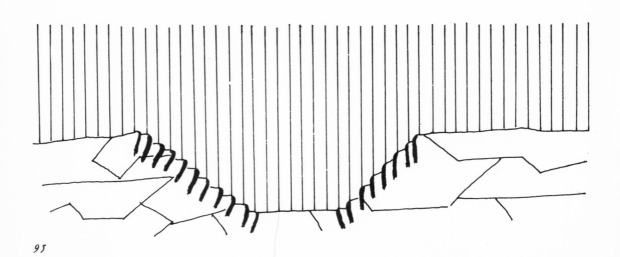

95

Correcting mistakes

Unfortunately mistakes do happen. In fig. *94* the black shape is to be changed. In order to avoid undoing all the other shapes right across the tapestry to the dotted line (1), which would take a long time, cut the weft at point (2) and undo it to point (3) (*95*). When this is finished undo the black shape and replace it by a different colour. Then weave in the adjoining shapes to their original size.

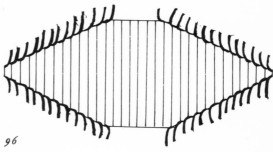

96

The same method can be applied whenever a shape has to be changed in the middle of the tapestry, either while still on the loom or off the loom (*96*). Instead of using the bobbin, thread the weft with a needle.

A common mistake is to leave out one or two warp ends, while passing the weft; this creates a float in the weft. Mostly the floats are on the right side of the tapestry. To correct this, using the same colour thread, darn in, with a needle, for about 1 in., following the pick to be mended. Leave about 1 in. of the fresh thread on each side on the wrong side and cut the float (*97*).

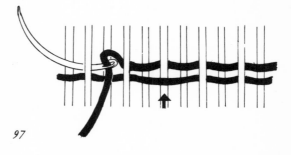

97

If there is a loose weft making a loop on the right side, pull it up from the wrong side.

In places where the warp is showing, due to insufficient beating down of the weft, darn in the same colour with a needle. Broken warp ends occur very seldom. It is easier to mend them if there are double ends and if only one of them breaks. To correct this run a needle along the warp end, overlapping the old warp end for about 1 in. With a single warp end more care must be taken to darn the new warp end through the right picks.

Combining tapestry weave with plain weave

Combining tapestry weave with plain weave gives the weaver great freedom. The warp is covered by the weft in some parts and shows in others according to the design. This suggests that the warp is not only a structure, on which the design is made entirely by the weft, but is a part of the design. The colour of the warp, as well as its texture, is important, therefore some thought must be given to choosing yarns for the warp (*98* and *99*). I find several thin yarns plied together more attractive than one thick strand. Two or three different colours and thicknesses and textures could be combined. Different kinds of yarn could be used for one warp end such as line and worsted, camel hair and linen, or cheviot and cotton.

The warp can be unevenly spaced if the design so requires it. The thickness of the warp ends could vary as well. There is no need for the weft to be of a uniform thickness. On the contrary, variation of different thicknesses of the weft gives a new dimension and different effects. The combination of a thick and thin yarn is part of the design. Where a thick yarn is used for the weft more of the warp can be seen, therefore the thicker the weft thread the more there will be seen of the warp, the thinner the weft the less of the warp is shown. This means that in one shape of the same weft colour, by variations of different thicknesses, a different colour or colour density can result. In places where a thinner yarn is used the warp will be covered completely, thus the colour of the weft will dominate. By adding more threads and making the weft thicker, more of the warp colour will be seen thus breaking the colour of the weft.

Another aspect in this type of tapestry results from uneven beating down of the weft. As in the orthodox woven tapestry the beating should be as even as possible, but the pressure on the weft can be varied. If more of the warp is to be shown the weft should be beaten down only slightly and in places where less is to be seen more pressure should be applied to the bobbin forcing the weft down. This will result in waviness of the weft. The weft will not always lie horizontally at a right angle to the warp and the picks will not always be parallel to each other.

98 'Landscape' detail, a combination of plain and tapestry weave. Most of the yarns have been hand-spun and different coloured wools have been mixed while carding. Yellow and brown weft, black worsted spun warp

99 'Seascape' natural colours of jute, hemp, camel
hair, horse hair and hand-spun wool dyed yellow
and brown

Because of the uneven thickness and the uneven beating down of the weft the spacing of the warp will differ as well. The thicker yarns in the weft and the looser the weave the more irregular the spacing of the warp ends will become. There is a certain wandering of the warp ends. It means that some warp ends will be drawn more closely together and some again will be pulled apart giving the appearance of streaks or irregular lines in the warp, which can be controlled and incorporated as part of the design.

The more regular the weave, that is by applying the appropriate thickness of the weft and even beating down, the more regular spacing of the warp ends. By adding thickness to the weft and by uneven beating down, irregular spacing of the warp will result. To bring the warp back to regular spacing, thinner weft threads and even beating down should be used again.

To join a fresh thread the procedure is the same as described on page 40, but if thicker yarns are used and the joining should occur in the more loosely woven parts, the fresh end of the weft should overlap the previous one for about 1 in. or 2 in. and in the case of several threads used in one pick, they should be staggered.

The free kind of tapestry gives the weaver the opportunity to use more unusual yarns such as horsehair and thick strings like jute and sisal, which would be less suitable for a more orthodox tapestry. These yarns are not very elastic and some of them would be too thick to cover the warp completely but in free tapestry this could be turned to advantage.

All these different yarns suggest a new approach to designing tapestry. In an orthodox tapestry the shapes are very definite, sharp and pointed; in the free tapestry the shapes are rounder and more wavy. Because of the uneven thickness in the weft or the warp and the different elasticity it is very difficult to keep an even tension and therefore the finished tapestry will not always hang com-

pletely straight and it is very difficult to avoid buckling in places. But this drawback should not be discouraging as many advantages will be gained, making the tapestry much more personal and giving unexpected results. In tapestry weave the warp ends are always straight and only the weft goes in a wavy manner around the warp ends (*100*). In plain weave not only is the weft wavy but also the

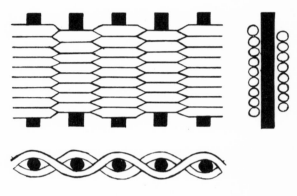

100

warp to a certain extent (*101*) which means that more warp will be used for plain weave and less for a tapestry weave. If, for instance, in one part of the hanging, more tapestry weave is used than plain weave, the warp will be longer in the former part of the warp. Because of this there will be less 'take up' of the warp. This type of tapestry should be designed in such a way that the 'take up' of the warp is balanced. Above a section of tapestry weave, plain weave should be used and vice versa, to bring the warp to the same length again.

The setting up of a frame or horizontal loom is similar to the methods already explained, only an adjustment should be made to vary the tension in the warp. It is easier to adjust the tension on frame III as described on page 33 by simply undoing the warp in sections and tightening it up again. On a frame with

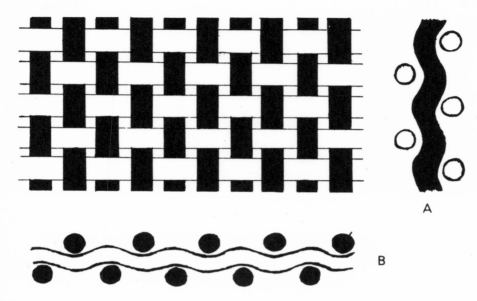

A

B

101

nails at the top and bottom, a piece of wood about 2 in. × 2 in. or 3 in. × 3 in. should be placed approximately 10 in. from the top of the frame, on the same side where the warp is wound. This will make the warp longer. If the tension, while weaving, becomes too tight, insert a thinner piece of wood in place of the one we had before, and repeat this each time the tension in the warp becomes too tight. Instead of one piece of wood 2 in. × 2 in. or 3 in. × 3 in., several sticks of $\frac{1}{4}$ in. thickness can be used which can later be taken out one by one, when the occasion arises (*102*). If the warp becomes looser and tighter in various places additional small pieces of wood can be added to obtain the correct tension.

If the tapestry hangs warp downwards a metal rod can be attached to the bottom of the hanging, either after the tapestry has been woven and while tying the fringes or it can be woven in at the beginning of weaving. The metal rod gives an extra weight which keeps the hanging taut.

The metal rod should be at least 2 in. longer than the width of the tapestry, so that it sticks out about 1 in. on each side. If steel or iron is used paint it beforehand with blackboard paint or flat black enamel which gives a matt finish and prevents rust.

To insert the metal rod, weave about 6 to 8 picks, put the rod through the next shed and start to weave the tapestry right above the rod. Because of the thickness of the rod there will be a slight gap between the rod and the weave; this can be adjusted when the hanging is taken off the loom, the rod being pushed up against the weaving and 6 or 8 picks could be pushed up very close to it.

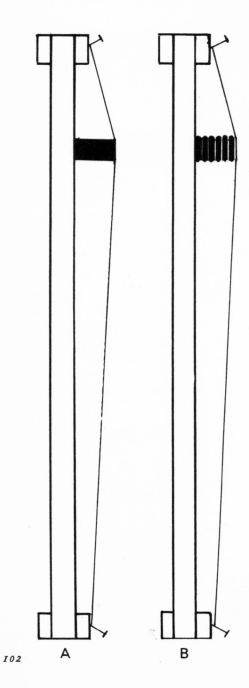

A   B

Woven weft

After weaving and designing rya rugs both as wall hangings and floor coverings I devised a method which would give a similar appearance to rya but in a flat weave. I started by weaving narrow strips which could then be woven together. The great advantage of this technique is that a more frequent change of colour is possible, it gives the weaver another dimension and also a different approach to designing. The technique itself suggests different forms and a different treatment of colours.

Making this tapestry is divided into two parts: first weaving strips and second weaving them together into a tapestry. To weave the strips make a warp of five ends, either using a warping frame, mill or simply by cutting a length of five threads, long enough for several strips. Use 6/8s lea linen, or 32/30s or 32/24s cotton twine or any strong thread; coloured if the warp is required to show. Wind the warp on a loom, preferably a two or four shaft foot loom, as it is quicker to weave. A table loom, inkle loom or frame can be used as well. Wind and set up the warp in the usual manner.

Space it through a 6 or 12 dents per inch reed, thus making the strips approximately ¾ in. wide (*103*). Wind some weft yarn on a small flat shuttle or simply cut the weft to 1 to 2 yard lengths. Pass the weft through the first shed, change the shed and pass the weft again, beating it down with the edge of the shuttle while the shuttle is still in the shed; or simply press the weft down with your fingers, using the reed from time to time. In order to join the next colour, overlap the fresh yarn over the last one under the centre two warp ends and cut each end of the weft to about ¼ in. after weaving about 1 in. or so (*103*). A 'woven weft' tapestry can hang either with the strips horizontally or vertically. If the strips are to lie horizontally an additional 1½ in. should be woven on each side of the strip, in a thinner yarn than the rest, for folding under. If the tapestry is to hang with the strips downwards, weave about 2 in. to 3 in. on one side (this is to make a pocket afterwards for a rod on which to hang the tapestry), and about ½ in. on the other side if the tapestry is to be finished with fringes or 1 in. to 1½ in.

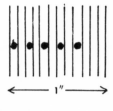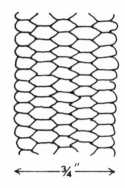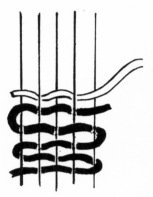

103

if it is to be folded under. Leave about a 6 in. interval in the warp between each strip. When taking the strips off the loom cut them leaving about 3 in. of warp on each side, knot the ends and attach a number to each strip, or pin each strip in the right order on a board, so as to know which strip should follow the next when weaving them together.

When the required number of strips has been woven make the warp for the actual tapestry. For this purpose I use 1/16s linen double or 2/28s linen single.

Spacing should be 8 ends per inch (8 double ends for 1/16s linen or 8 single ends for 2/28s): add 8 threads for each selvedge.

Weave about ½ in. to 1 in. before inserting the first strip. Always weave at least two picks between each strip. It will depend on the design as to how much of the weft should show between each strip.

Any yarns can be used both for the strips and for weaving them together again. The thickness of the yarns will depend on how much warp should be either covered or shown.

Before weaving the strips I draw the outlines of the design on strong tracing or grease-proof paper. Divide and cut the paper into narrow strips about 1 in. wide. The paper strips can be placed under the warp while weaving.

This type of tapestry imposes restrictions but on the other hand gives many new possibilities. Because it is difficult to get continuous shapes or lines exactly in the same places and on the same level in each strip it requires shapes and colours which merge from one into the other without definite outlines. The final warp does not need to be of a uniform colour. Because it is possible to have a different colour in the warp and weft, in the strips and in the final warp and weft between the strips, there can be many colours crossing and interchanging, giving the hanging a great richness both in colour and tone (*104* and *105*).

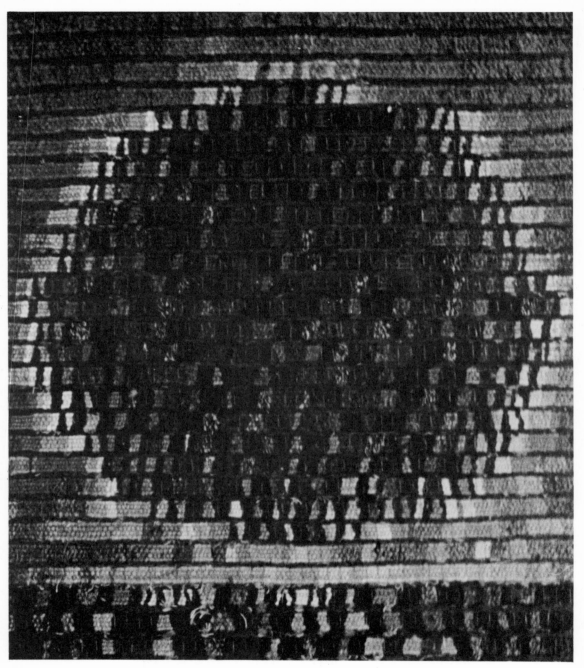

104 'Moon' *red and dark blue. Weft woven tapestry*

105 Detail

Warp and weft face

The orthodox tapestry is a weft face or weft rib fabric. The opposite to weft rib weave is the warp face or warp rib weave (*106*). In the warp rib the warp is spaced very closely, covering the weft entirely. In the *Dovecote* I combined these two rib weaves (*108* and *109*). In some parts of the hanging the warp is showing and the weft is covered and in others the weft is visible and the warp is hidden by the weft. To weave this type of tapestry it is essential to have a four shaft (harness) loom (or more shafts (harnesses)).

Warp In the *Dovecote* I used 14 cut cheviot, but any yarns suitable for warp can be used.

Weft Mainly cheviot, worsted and cotton fancy yarns.

Spacing 24 double ends to the inch.

Drafting 4, 3, 4, 3, 4, 3 and 2, 1, 2, 1, 2, 1 (*107*).

Tying of pedals. Tie first and third shafts (harnesses) to one pedal, second and fourth shafts (harnesses) to the second pedal; first and second shafts (harnesses) to the third pedal and the third and fourth shafts (harnesses) to the fourth pedal (*109*).

Weaving Lift shafts 1 and 3, and 2 and 4 alternately for the warp rib, and 1 and 2, and 3 and 4 for the weft rib. A change from warp rib to weft rib and vice versa can be made at any point of the hanging.

To get the full benefit of this method the tapestry should be designed in such a way that the warp rib is more dominant.

Due to uneven 'take up' the warp will be longer in some places and shorter in others; that is in the parts where more warp rib weave is woven, more of the warp will be used and

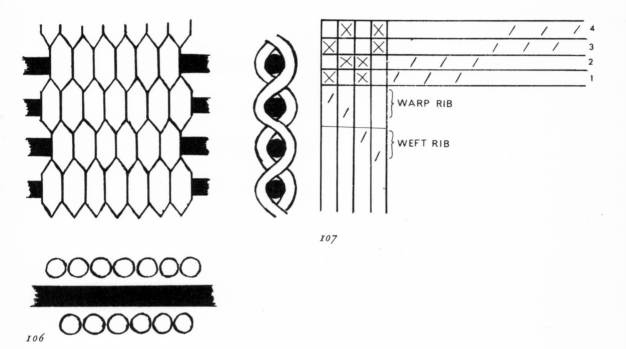

WARP RIB

WEFT RIB

106

so the warp will become shorter. Where weft rib is woven the warp will be longer. Therefore the tension in the warp must be corrected from time to time. If the warp is tied on the back of the loom, nearest to the back roller, re-adjusting the warp is fairly easy. If the warp is tied to the front of the loom use sticks for correcting the tension; the sticks should be placed at the back of the warp in different sections, according to the uneven tension.

108 '*Dovecote*' *warp and weft face tapestry. Light*
green on navy blue background. Use of novelty
varns

Some details about *Dovecote*

The warp was made in sections, but beamed together. Sections A, B, C, D were made of similar colours, sections E, F, G of light colours. In sections E, F and G, I changed the light colour, towards the end, to the dark colour, that of the background sections A, B, C, D; sections E and G show where the colour changes (*110*). To change the colours while making a warp can only be done if double thread has been used as one warp end (*111*). Make the warp in the usual way, using preferably a warping frame. At the point of changing colours loop both threads round each other and return with one colour to the first peg and the other to the last peg.

To avoid slits in the tapestry I wove the weft yarn in the warp rib for a ½ in. or more into the weft rib.

A   E   B   F   C   G   D

110

111

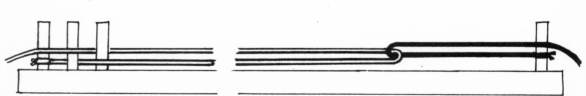

Double-cloth weave

Although not a tapestry weave this weave is nearest in appearance to it. A hanging woven in double-cloth weave is quicker to weave provided the weft thread is woven right across the whole width, from one selvedge to the other. If the weft is woven in sections it would take just as long to weave as ordinary tapestry or even longer. The design is made with two different colours woven at the same time. Whichever colour is visible on one side, the other colour is visible on the other side (*112* and *113*). This makes the fabric reversible if all ends are woven in. Changing colours is carried out in horizontal strips. Therefore a gradual changing of colours and tones is more suitable for this technique. A two shaft (harness) foot loom (or more shafts) (harnesses) is necessary for this weave.

Warp and weft yarns Similar to the warp and weft yarns as described for tapestry.

Spacing 8 single ends per inch, or 6 and 4 ends for a coarser hanging.

Drafting 2, space, 1, space and so on, which means that every other thread goes through the space between the two heddles, and is not threaded. Every other end goes either through the eyelet of the heddle of the second or the first shaft (harness) (*114*). On a four shaft (harness) loom the draft would be 4, space, 3, space, 2, space, 1, space, and so on. The lifting of the shafts (harnesses) would be 1 and 3 and 2 and 4 (*115*), or in order to get a better shed the draft could be 4, space, 2, space, 3, space, 1, space, and so on; the lifting of the shafts (harnesses) would be 1 and 2, 3 and 4. The idea of having every other thread going through a space and not being threaded is that when one shaft is lifted and the other lowered (1 and 3, and 2 and 4 or 1 and 2 or 3 and 4 on four shaft (harness) looms), the warp ends which have not been threaded through any heddles stay on one level, thus creating two sheds at the same time, sheds A and B (*116*). The shuttle with one colour, say black, is passed through the top shed A, over C warp, white thread through the other shed B, under C warp. After changing the shed, the black weft could be passed again through the

112

113

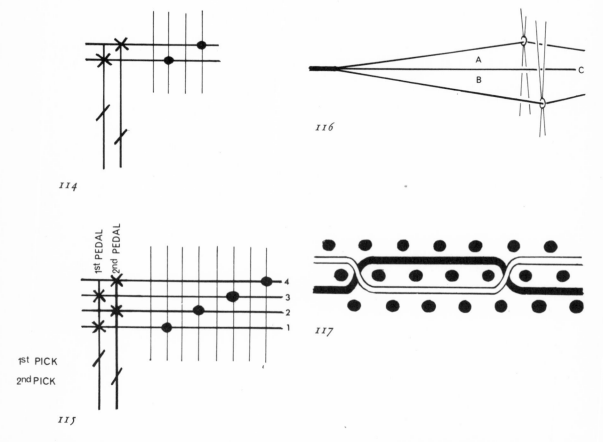

114

116

1st PEDAL
2nd PEDAL

4
3
2
1

1st PICK
2nd PICK

115

117

top shed and the white through the bottom shed, if continued the black would be visible on one side, that is on the top, and the white would be underneath. In order to reverse the order and thus have the black underneath and the white on top, put the black through the lower shed B, and the white through the top shed A.

If the colours are changed in the middle or at any other point, that is passing from shed A to B and consequently from B to A, any simple shape can be made. Change of the two colours can be done at any point, but wherever the black yarn is passed through the top shed A, the white must be passed through the ower shed B and vice versa (*117*).

96

Rya rugs as wall hangings

Rya is a Scandinavian term applied to long tufted rugs. Originally rya rugs were used in the Scandinavian countries as bedcovers as well as floor coverings and wall hangings. Nowadays rya is mainly used as a floor covering and wall hanging.

The colours in rya can be mixed very freely and give an appearance of great richness and depth. Because it is three-dimensional the light falls at a different angle on each single thread changing colours from light to dark. To weave a rya a foot loom, upright loom or frame can be used. Setting up of the loom or frame is similar to the methods described for tapestries. If a frame is used, method III is the best for this purpose. Cotton twine or linen can be used for the warp.

If the spacing of the warp is 4 or less ends per inch, double warp ends should be used. If 6 or 8 ends per inch use single warp ends. As there are 2 warp ends needed for each tuft and 2, or 4 warp ends on each side for a border

(*118*) the number of warp ends must be counted accordingly.

Start to weave exactly as for a tapestry. The thickness of the weft will vary according to the spacing of the warp. The coarser the spacing, the thicker the weft. For 4 ends per inch use 2 to 3 threads of 2 ply carpet wool; for 6 ends per inch use 2 threads and for 8 ends per inch 1 thread of 2 ply carpet wool. Weave 1 in. or 2 in. if the rug is to be finished with fringes or about 4 in. for folding under.

The thickness of the yarn for the tufts is determined by the spacing of the warp. If 2 ply carpet wool is used for tufts, take 8 threads to make tufts for 4 ends per inch spaced warp, 6 threads for 6 ends per inch and 4 threads for 8 ends per inch. If other yarns are used one can find out what thickness to use by experiment. If the yarn is not thick enough gaps will show between each knot. If the yarn is too thick it will result in buckling.

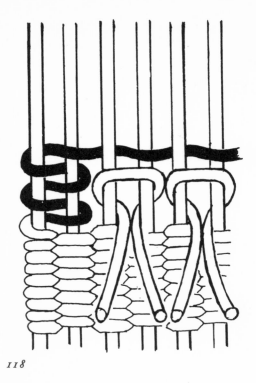
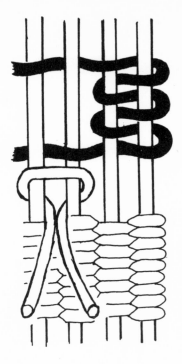

118

Knotting

Method I

Prepare the yarn for the tufts by winding it into a ball. Leave the first 2, 4 or more warp ends (this will depend on the width of the border) and start with the first warp end, after the border, on the left side of the rug. Take the end of the yarn under the first warp end, starting from the right side, then over the first and second warp end, bring it forward between the two ends and below the knot and pull it down. While pulling it down regulate the length of the tuft by either pulling more on the right side or the left side and cut it to the required length (*119*). Do not pull the knot too tightly, otherwise the spacing of the warp will be affected. Continue to make the knots either continuously from one side to the other or according to the design, knotting some colours first and then the others. The knot described is known as the Turkish or Ghiordes knot. The same knot is used in most hand-knotted rugs and carpets.

While knotting, all the warp ends should be on the same level, that is when the shed is closed. This method is the best one, especially when only a few tufts of one colour are required at a time, because it is quick and easy to change from one colour to another. It is also easy to vary the length of the tufts if so required. The length of the tufts can vary from 1 in. to 3 in. and more. It is determined by the design and the amount of tapestry weave woven between each row of tufts; the more tapestry weave between each row of tufts the longer the length of tufts, which should cover about two-thirds of the last row of tufts (*120*).

119

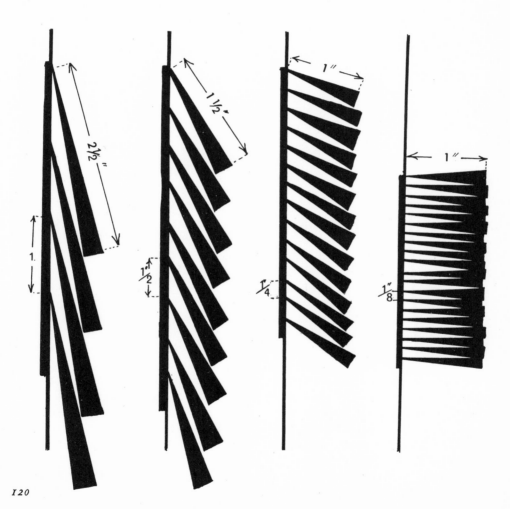

120

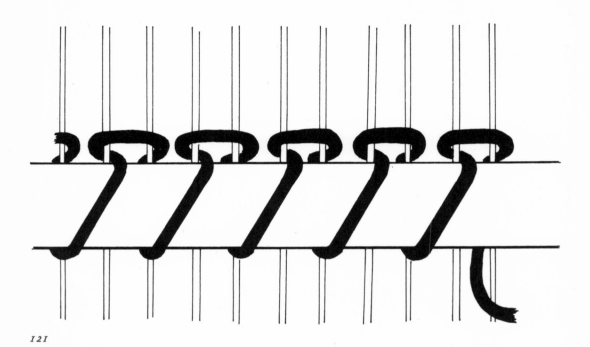

121

Method II

The knot is the same as described above, but the method is different. The yarn for tufts should be wound on a small flat shuttle. Instead of going round the warp ends with the 'short length' and cutting each tuft separately, the 'long length' is used, that is the shuttle with the whole length wound on it does the manipulating. Take the shuttle from the right side to the left under the first warp end leaving the short end in front, take over this one and the next warp end under it and between the two ends. Place a stick, 1 in. or more wide, in position across the warp, and put the yarn round the stick; make another knot, looping the yarn round the stick (*121*). When a whole row of tufts is finished, cut the loops. A special wooden gauge can be made or bought to make the cutting of the loops easier. This method is very useful if a uniform length of tufts has to be maintained and if a colour change does not occur too often. The length of the tufts would be the width of the stick or gauge, therefore for different length of tufts different widths of the stick or gauge must be used.

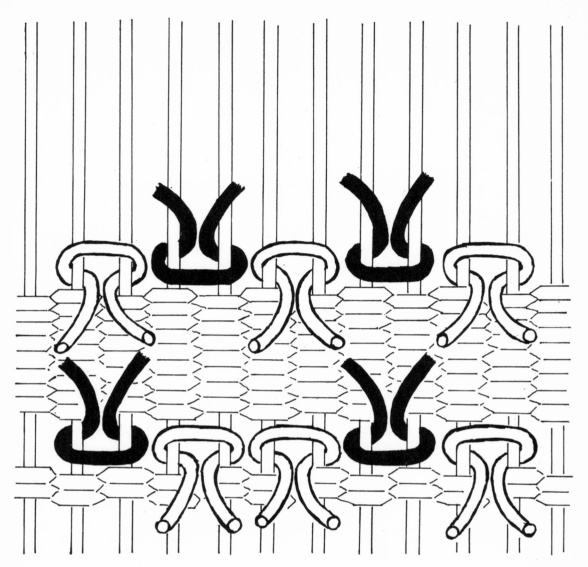

122

Method III

The yarn for the tufts could be cut beforehand into short lengths using the Turkish knot. To get an even length of yarn wrap it round a gauge and then cut it along the edge of the gauge.

After each row of tufts weave 6 picks on one side for the border, thus building up to the level of the knots. Then pass the weft to the other side. Before passing the weft make sure that it goes through the next shed to the previous one, which is under the knots. Weave the weft for 6 picks again, using the outside warp ends which are meant for the border (*118*). Then weave $\frac{1}{2}$ in. to 1 in. or more, using tapestry weave between each row of tufts. The spacing between each row of tufts will depend on how close the tufts are to be. The closer the spacing, the greater the density of tufts. The width of the spacing will affect not only the density but also the angle of the tufts. The wider the space the flatter will the tufts lie (*120*). After the last row of tufts weave 1 in. to 2 in. if finishing with fringes or 4 in. to 6 in.—enough to make a 'pocket'—through which a stick could be put for hanging the rug. The last row of tufts will show all the knots. To prevent the knots from showing, reverse the procedure of knot making in the last rows as follows so that the ends of the tufts will point to the other side, thus covering the knots: Start with the fourth row from last. Reverse every fourth knot, then reverse every third knot in the third row from last, every second in the second row from last and reverse all the knots in the last row (*122*). Most of the original Finnish rya-rugs are woven with a special mixture of wool, the spacing of the warp is 8 ends per inch, that is 4 tufts per inch and only $\frac{1}{2}$ in. of tapestry weave is woven between each row of tufts.

Designing

As practically every tuft could be of a different colour it is very easy to change from one colour to another, which gives great freedom to the designer. In rya there are less limitations in regard to shapes, but it is very easy to over-estimate the number of workable shapes and only by working it out on squared paper can the changes in colours and shapes be assessed. And of course the more shapes and different colours the longer it takes to weave. Lines, unlike in tapestry, look better if they are vertical, that is running along the warp. Technically it is easy to weave them both vertically or horizontally, only the appearance of the vertical lines is smoother and more interesting than the horizontal ones which look clumsy. Each tuft can have several threads not only of different colours but of different thickness and texture. It is very easy to mix let us say linen with wool, or knots can be made with unspun wool, jute or flax.

The length of tufts can vary. By different lengths, shapes can be distorted and show more of one colour and less of another. The tufts can be in certain parts only or long tufts and short tufts can be combined with narrower or wider spacing between each row of tufts in one hanging.

To put the design on paper use a squared paper, painting the colours either in transparent paint or drawing symbols for each colour (*123*). The design, drawn to scale, can be squared up. Each square on the paper should represent 2 tufts in the rug. For example if the spacing is 8 ends to the inch, there will be 4 tufts to the inch. Between each row of tufts there is $\frac{1}{2}$ in. of tapestry weave: $\frac{1}{2}$ in. square in the rug will be equal to a square on the design, that is 2 tufts per square equals 2 tufts ($\frac{1}{2}$ in. square) in the rug.

If the spacing is 4 ends per inch, that is 2 tufts per inch and 1 in. of tapestry weave between each row of tufts, each 1 in. square in the rug will be 2 tufts and similarly, each square on the design paper will represent 2 tufts.

123

Other kinds of wall hangings

In recent years more and more weavers are becoming interested in an experimental and free kind of woven wall hanging such as 'Rams Head' (*131*). Many are developing their own ideas and the results are both fascinating and stimulating. Some of the hangings can be woven on frames and, in fact, some types of hangings can only be woven on frames. The following description is how to weave hangings similar to *Moon* (*127*) and *Twin Constellation* (*128*).

Warp 1/12s lea linen.

Spacing 8 ends per inch. (Double ends for the selvedge.)

Weft 1/12s lea linen, coarse spun linen, hemp, jute, camel and horsehair, unspun flax, hemp and jute; wood veneer; X-ray films with honesty seeds.

Setting up of the frame See page 23. A wooden piece should be placed under the warp for correcting the tension (*102*).

Weaving Start to weave about 3 in. to 4 in. from the bottom, leaving enough of the warp for fringes. Weave about 6 picks of 1/12s linen, wound on a long, flat shuttle. Beat down the weft with the edge of the shuttle, while the shuttle is in the shed. After the sixth pick insert a metal rod, about 2 in. longer than the width of the hanging and about $\frac{1}{4}$ in. in diameter. The rod should be painted with blackboard paint (flat black enamel) beforehand to prevent rusting. Brass or copper rods can be used. After inserting the metal rod weave another 8 to 10 picks, beating down the weft with the edge of the flat shuttle. After this use a tapestry bobbin for forcing down the weft. The weft then should not be beaten down too closely, plenty of space being left between each pick. Beat down the weft only in some places, giving the weft a free flowing line. Weave a thin linen weft all along the hanging, in plain weave; all other yarns are inserted additionally, using the same shed as the 1/12s linen. The edges of the veneer, used in the hanging, are burned to remove sharp edges and splinters and also to add colour and texture. The honesty seeds are put between two pieces of X-ray film which are glued together with polyvinylacetate (PVA), a transparent glue. Any other seeds or leaves could be inserted. The hanging is finished in a manner similar to the beginning. A bamboo stick can be inserted instead of the metal rod. Before cutting the hanging off the frame it should be treated with PVA. Apply PVA with a wide brush, brushing it very sparingly all over the hanging, leave it to dry and then cut it off finishing the ends of the warp with fringes.

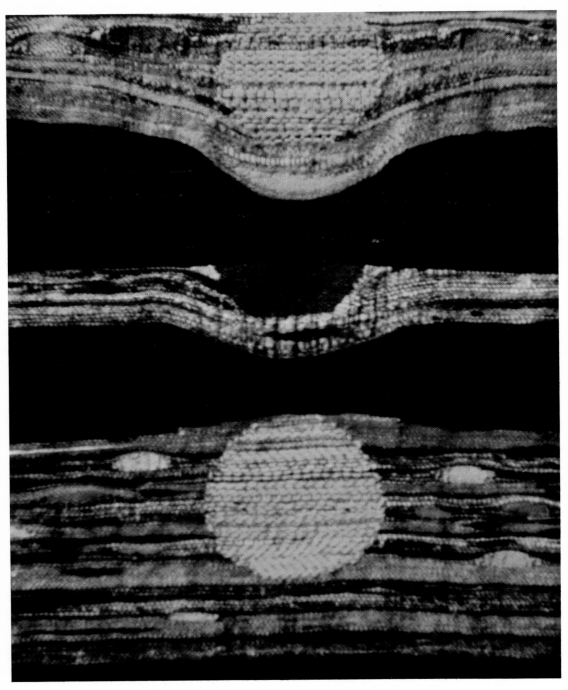

Detail of a plain and tapestry weave.
Warp: black worsted, Weft: hand-spun wool

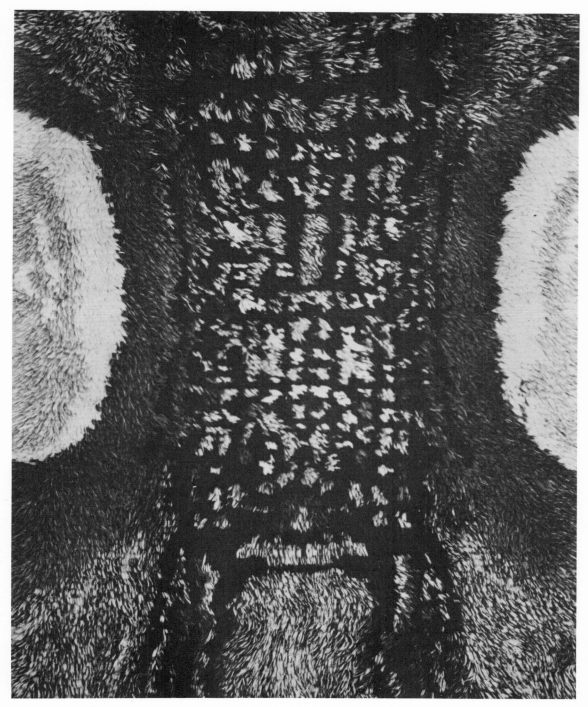

124 '*Sunset*' *rya. Range of light and dark reds*

125 '*Autumn*' *detail of rya, deep purple, blue and green*

Designing

This chapter deals with the possibilities and restrictions of tapestry design. Before starting to design find out first what the tapestry is for, and how it is to be made. It would be wrong to start off with designing on paper and then interpreting the design which is carried out in different media into a tapestry. Before putting down the image on paper first weave at least one small tapestry, developing the image while weaving. Only then when more of the properties of tapestry weaving are grasped can the image be put on paper first and woven afterwards. On the other hand I do not intend to give too many strict rules as to what makes a good tapestry design, because all the 'do's and don't's' are, I think, too restricting. The problem of designing must be approached with a fresh, open mind without preconceived ideas. Some traditional concepts of designing tapestry can be accepted or disregarded. But one thing cannot be disregarded; the fundamental technical properties and their restrictions which are imposed on the tapestry designer. Even now tapestry is regarded by many people as a medium akin to painting and

it is thought any good painter can supply a design for it. This is a fallacy which surrounds this craft more than any other, probably because it is nearer to painting or mural painting. But then who should design a tapestry? a weaver? Probably many weavers could weave a tapestry but not design one. I divide tapestries into three categories: those designed by painters, those designed by weavers and those designed by tapestry designers. All of these groups have produced and are producing wonderful tapestries and, on the other hand, very bad ones. Let us take the first group. Most of the past and present tapestries were, and still are, designed by painters. Painters have been and still are asked to do this because there is no one else, or if there is, they have not the fame and popularity of the painter. Some designs produced by painters are more suitable for a tapestry than others. But even if the image is suitable and the design itself a work of art, very seldom is the tapestry a work of art as well. The painter creates his colours and shapes in paint, and the quality and texture of wool or any other yarns are often disregarded. A knowledge of different weaves or different weave structures and the use of the warp as part of the design is unknown to him. The second group, those of the weavers who have the knowledge of yarns and the technical possibilities seldom have the imagination, personality and potentiality of the painter. The result is often a woven wall hanging which is not always an interesting tapestry. A combination of the qualities of the two previous groups makes the tapestry designer. A combination of the knowledge of the weaver and the imagination of the painter can result in good tapestry. A tapestry is neither a painting nor merely a weaving. It is a craft on its own. A tapestry is mainly a wall hanging, which means it should be decorative but not in the sense as wallpaper or fabric printing is decorative. It is individual and has a design which is restricted within the specific shape and not a repetitive pattern.

Size

Originally tapestries were woven in small sizes. Only since the fourteenth century have the French and Flemish tapissiers started to weave large tapestries and these have come to be regarded as large hangings covering huge, empty walls. Large tapestries are woven in big ateliers, where several weavers can work at the same time on one tapestry. No individual weaver can afford the time to weave a very large tapestry as even on a fairly coarse spaced warp and of a simple design, it takes an experienced person to weave as much as a square foot a day. This means that to weave a tapestry of say 10 ft × 14 ft an individual weaver would spend from 140 to 160 working days, not taking into account such things as designing or the dyeing of yarns. Only medium and small size tapestries can therefore be woven by the

individual weaver. Naturally small tapestries require different treatment in design than the large ones and the standard and quality do not need to suffer because of the size. To criticise a tapestry because of size is a fallacy; the size is not important—it is the design itself which should decide if a tapestry is good or not. Formerly only the very rich people who lived in castles, palaces and large mansions could afford to buy tapestries, hence the sizes were large. Today only commercial or public buildings can afford large spaces for tapestries.

Shapes

I would advise the beginner to start with a small tapestry. After weaving the sampler, the first tapestry should be the extension of the sampler in order to find out, for example, what shapes are the easiest and most natural to weave. All the shapes and lines running across the warp are easier to weave than the vertical ones, which run along the warp (*132* to *134*).

Lines

It is better to avoid any thin lines running along the warp. The thinnest vertical line that can be woven is the thickness of one warp end, that is if the warp is spaced 8 ends per inch, the thinnest line will be 1/8 in. The weft cannot simply be taken round and round a warp end as this would result in slits on both sides of the line giving a very poor structure. To avoid this it is necessary to link it at least on one side to the adjoining shape. Changing the direction of the line can be done by stepping. On the other hand, lines running horizontally or near to horizontal across the warp are very easy to weave.

126 'Winter' *detail of rya, black and white*

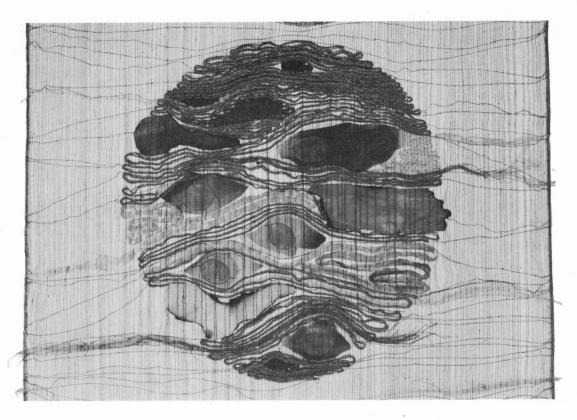

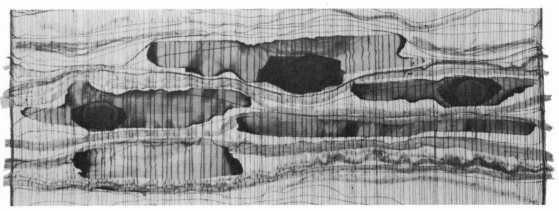

127 'Moon' *details, natural colours*

128 'Twin Constellation' *natural colours*

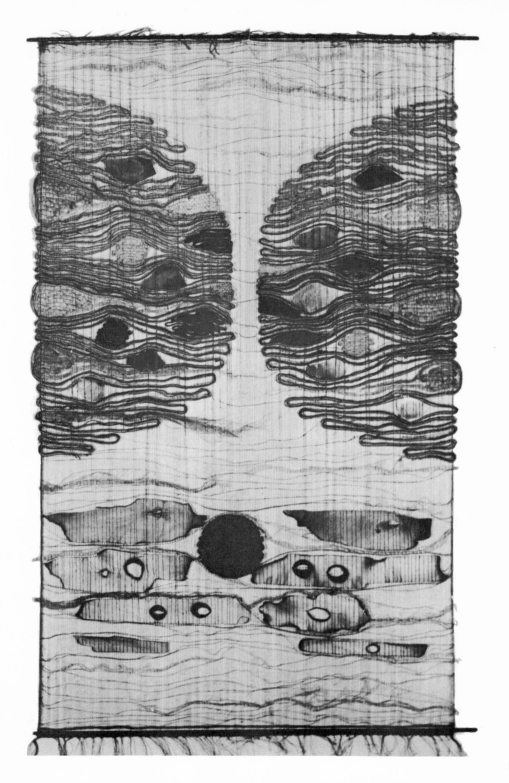

III

Colours

In painting, varied density of colour can be obtained with one brush-stroke and by applying different pressure. Mixing two or more colours in oil paint or water-colour will also produce a great variety of colours and tones. In tapestry the colour is more limited and is basically flat. If the same colour thread, let us say red, is used in one shape, the colour will be the same in all parts of the shape. The even distribution of the colour can be changed by:

(1) plying two or more threads of different colours or shades. For example if red is plyed with a blue thread, the result will be red and blue spots giving the impression of purple, similar to the technique of the pointillist painters. Because of the irregular twisting of both yarns, in some places either the red or the blue will be more dominant:

(2) uneven dyeing of the yarn which will give an irregular distribution of the colour thus breaking flatness of the shape. If the weaver dyes his own yarns, uneven dyeing can be an advantage. This happens if a great deal of yarn is put into a small container, preventing the dye evenly penetrating the yarns. The same dyed yarn can be put into different dye baths. For example, dye first unevenly in yellow, and then re-dye red. In places where the yellow is more intense, it will change into orange and in the other parts the yarn will be more red. Uneven dyeing can result by tying or knotting some parts of the yarn:

(3) plying novelty yarns, of two or more different colours and textures. Two or more threads can be plyed on the spinning wheel and by applying different tension to each thread they will twist unevenly. For example, if black and white threads are used, pull more on the black thread and keep the white thread loose, this will result in the white thread twisting round the black thread, practically covering it, reverse the procedure and the black will show more.

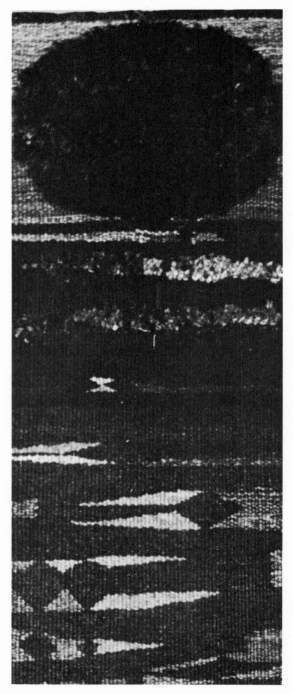

129 'Moon II' deep blue, light blue and green, partly tufted. Cotton warp

130 'Reflection' *khaki green and greyish brown screens, partly tufted. Cotton warp*

(4) spinning your own thread, mixing either two or more colours while carding, or mixing different kinds of raw materials before spinning.

(5) hatching as described on page 61, and other possibilities on page 60.

In small and medium-size tapestries I would suggest avoiding great contrasts in colours; rather have a wide range of similar colours, contrasting light and dark, warm and cold of the same colour. For example a blue can range from a very warm purplish blue to an acidy greenish blue. Try to make a small tapestry appear large and with one unity and not to divide it into small, separate shapes and colours.

Putting the image on paper

Only after you have had the experience of weaving at least one small tapestry without any elaborate design should ideas be put down on paper first. For a tapestry I am to weave myself, I prefer to make very rough sketches, but if it is to be woven by someone else a more detailed sketch is necessary. In the latter case I first make a few small sketches and then a drawing to full scale, only outlining the shapes and numbering them for colours.

While working on one tapestry, the idea for another often comes as an extension of the tapestry on which I am working. I seldom try out the colours in paint, preferring to select the colours in yarns. I usually make a collection of all the possible yarns I could use and play around with the colours and textures, by adding or taking some away, and how I am going to ply and mix them. I sometimes cut a piece of cardboard and wind a few inches of the yarns round it, winding more of one colour, less of another in proportions similar to those to be used in the tapestry. If a client commissions a tapestry and asks for a design beforehand, I try to make the design look as much like the finished tapestry as possible, as it is difficult for someone else to visualize the end product. For a coloured design I use oil paint diluted with turpentine. This gives the best results, as the colours, even when superimposed, retain their transparency. Pastels can be used for designing tapestry with good results too. Whichever method in designing is applied, either by painting in oil, tempera, water-colours, pastels or collage (paper or textile collage), the ability to visualize the end product is of main importance. In a design not only has the technique to be taken into account but also the standard of art values at the time. What was original some years ago cannot be repeated today. Even if styles and moods re-occur, they are always different, re-created and reborn. A new direction in art, on the other hand, is probably not so important as the artist himself and what and how he is creating. But styles bring fresh ideas and new problems to solve.

131 'Ram's Head' *natural colours, jute, hemp, camel hair and willow*

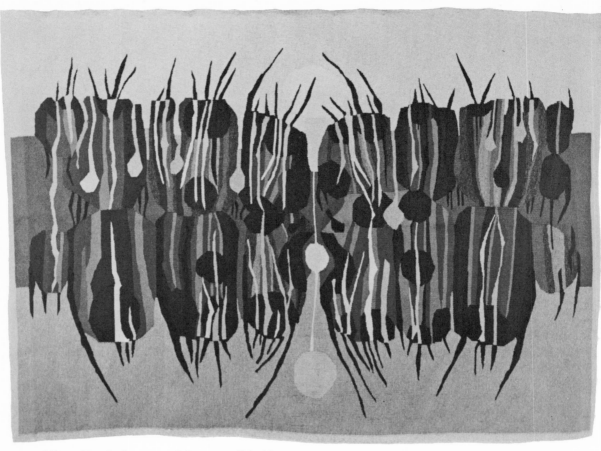

132 'Growth' dark green and brown on light blue
and green background. Tapestry woven sideways. Cotton warp

Detail of 'Growth'

133 'Forest' black on deep blue. Tapestry woven sideways. Cotton warp

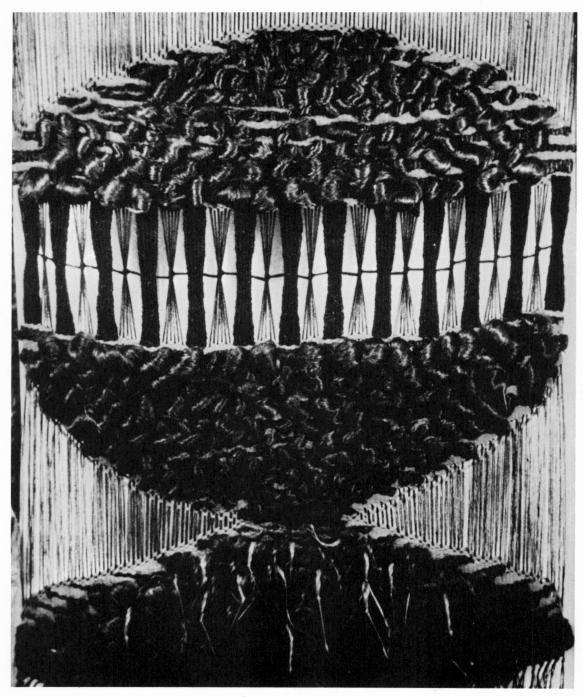

134 'Autumn Moon'. Warp: black mohair. Weft: red carpet wool and
dyed dressed (unspun) jute (black, deep purple, mauve, blue)

118

Glossary

Batten	A wooden frame holding the reed on horizontal looms (and some vertical ones).
Beater	A wooden or metal comb-like tool used for forcing the weft down.
Bobbin	A wooden spool on which the weft is wound. The pointed tip of the bobbin is used for packing the weft down.
Cartoon	A design painted or drawn to a full scale. A recent method is to outline the shapes in black and number the colours.
Cross sticks or Shed sticks	Two long wooden laths securing the cross.
Dent	Space in the reed.
Dentage	The number of dents per inch.
End	A single warp thread.
Flat sticks	Long wooden laths used for beaming the warp and used at the start of weaving.
G Clamp (C Clamp)	G-shaped metal clamp.
Heddle	A loop of cotton twine or wire with a centre loop through which the warp end is passed.
Inkle loom	A narrow, frame-like loom for weaving braids.
Kelim (Khilim, Kilim)	A flat rug in tapestry weave, of oriental origin.
Lea	A yardage measurement of linen.
Leash	A single loop of cotton twine used instead of a heddle on a frame.
Pick	A single weft thread.

Reed	A steel comb-like implement for spacing out the warp and beating down the weft.
Rod	A dowel, one inch or more in diameter separating the even from the uneven warp ends.
Rod shed	Shed created by the rod.
Rya	Scandinavian name for a long tufted rug.
Selvedge	The edge of a web. In tapestry usually two or more threads on each side.
Shaft	Two wooden laths on which the heddles are looped.
Shed	The opening in the warp through which the weft passes.
Shuttle	A tool for carrying and passing the weft through the shed.
Temple or Tenterhooks	A wooden implement to keep an even width while weaving.
Tensioner	Implement to release and tighten tension of the warp.
Warp	Threads running lengthways.
Web	A piece of weaving.
Weft	Threads woven across the warp.

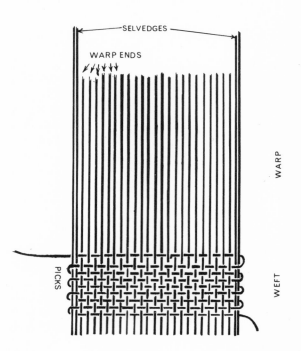

Bibliography

Key to Weaving	Mary E. Black, The Bruce Publishing Co., Milwaukee 1945 A book of hand weaving techniques, useful for beginners
Embroidery and Tapestry-Weaving	A. H. Cristie, Artistic Craft Series of Handbooks, Pitman
Your Yarn Dyeing	Elsie G. Davenport, Sylvan Press
A Book of Tapestries	W. & B. Forman, Spring Books
Woven Rugs	Ronald Grierson, Dryad Press, Leicester Describes Kelim techniques woven on frame which is very similar to tapestry weaving
Swiss Medieval Tapestries	F. Gysin, Batsford
Handloom Weaving	Luther Hooper, Pitman Useful for beginners
The Dyeing of Textile Fibres	R. S. Horsfall, and L. G. Lawrie, Chapman and Hall
French Tapestry	A. Lejard, Paul Elek An interesting chapter on tapestry technique
Designing Tapestry	Jean Lurçat, Rockliff
A History of Tapestry	W. G. Thompson, Hodder and Stoughton
Contemporary Tapestry	Harriet Tidball, Shuttle Craft Monograph Twelve 1964. Distributed by Craft and Hobby service, Big Sur, California Deals with tapestry techniques

The Textile Arts	Verla Birrell, Harper and Brothers, New York, 1959
Decorative Wall Hangings	David B. Van Dommelen, Funk and Wagnalls Company Inc., New York 1962
The Art and Craft of Hand Weaving	Lili Blumenau, Crown Publishers, New York, 1955
On Weaving	Anni Albers, Wesleyan University Press, Middletown, Connecticut 1965
The Technique of Weaving	John Tovey, Batsford 1965

Suppliers

Great Britain

Yarns, looms, frames	Dryad Handicrafts Ltd, Northgate, Leicester
Books on weaving, Swedish tapestry yarns	K. R. Drummond, 30 Hart Grove, Ealing Common, London W5
Woollen yarns	T. M. Hunter, Sutherland, Wool Mill, Brora, Scotland
	Robert Laidlaw and Sons, Seafield Mills, Keith, Scotland
Frames made to order, bobbins, looms	Harris Looms, North Grove Road, Hawkhurst, Kent
Brussels wool	Jackson's Store, Croft Mill, Hebden Bridge, Yorkshire
Horse hair, camel hair, grey and white wool yarns	The Multiple Fabric Co Ltd, Dudley Hill, Bradford 4
Worsted	J. Marsden, 46 Speeton Avenue, Bradford 7
Horizontal and vertical foot looms	Maxwell John, Folders Lane, Burgess Hill, Sussex
32/30s, 32/24s, cotton twine	J. & W. Stuart Ltd, Esk Mills, Musselburgh, Scotland
Chemical dyes	Skilbeck Brothers, 55–57, Glengall Road, London SE15

United States of America

Tapestry and rug yarns, tapestry looms, cotton twine — Paternayan Brothers Inc., 312 East 95 Street, New York City

Woollen yarns, linen, silk, rayon, novelty cotton — Shuttlecraft of Rhode Island, P.O. Box 6041, Providence 4, Rhode Island

Charles Y. Butterworth, 222 E. Susquehanna Avenue, Philadelphia 25, Pennsylvania

Yarn Depot, 545 Suttur Street, San Francisco, California

Contessa, P.O. Box 37, Lebanon, Connecticut, 06249

Home Yarns Company, 862 Avenue of the Americas, New York 10001, New York

Woollen yarns — Tranquillity Studio, West Cornwall, Connecticut

The Silver Shuttle, 1301 35 Street, Washington, D.C.

Swedish yarns, frame looms — House of Kleen, P.O. Box 326, Stonington, Connecticut

Linens — Frederick J. Fawcett, 129 South Street, Boston, 11, Massachusetts

Weaving flutes, shuttles, combs for tapestry — Edward Bosworth, 132 Indian Creek Road, Ithaca, New York

Winding bobbins — Edward Bosworth, 132 Indian Creek Road, Ithaca, New York